# WEE TROUPIE

## THE ALEC TROUP STORY

# WEE TROUPIE

## THE ALEC TROUP STORY

*David W. Potter*

The
History
Press

First published in 2002 by Tempus Publishing Limited

Reprinted in 2010 by
The History Press
The Mill, Brimscombe Port,
Stroud, Gloucestershire, GL5 2QG
www.thehistorypress.co.uk

British Library Cataloguing in Publication Data.
A catalogue record for this book is available from the British Library.

ISBN 978 0 7524 2411 8

Typesetting and origination by Tempus Publishing.
Printed and bound in England.

# CONTENTS

About the Author           6

Acknowledgements           7

Introduction           8

1      Forfar: The Early Years           9

2      The Emerging Genius           23

3      Dundee           37

4      Troup in the Troops           47

5      Après la Fin de la Guerre           51

6      Everton           78

7      Troupie and Dixie: The *Annus Mirabilis*, 1927/28           97

8      Return of a Hero, 1930-33           109

9      Scotland           128

10      The Twilight of the God           149

# ABOUT THE AUTHOR

David Potter is sixty-two years old and lives in Kirkcaldy, although he was born and brought up in Forfar, hence his interest in Alec Troup. He has written more than twenty books on football and cricket. He is a semi-retired teacher, having worked at Glenrothes High School for thirty-two years before working in a part-time capacity at Osborne House, Dysart. Other than football his interests are cricket, drama, the poetry of Robert Burns and walking his dog. He is married, has three grown-up children and three grandchildren.

# ACKNOWLEDGEMENTS

I would like to acknowledge the help I have received from many people in compiling this book, particularly from Brian Taylor, the grandson of Alec Troup. Brian's charming wife, Celia, has also been very hospitable and friendly. Help has also been forthcoming from Betty Piggott and May Stewart (Alec's nieces) and their respective husbands; Alec Herd, who sent me photographs; Allan Stewart, who worked with Alec in Brechin during the Second World War. Norrie Price, the author of *Up Wi The Bonnets* and *They Wore the Dark Blue* was also very helpful, as was Duncan Carmichael, who gave me information on Alec's few appearances for Ayr United. George 'Pud' Hill, himself a good player for Dundee in the early 1950s, told me about the day of Troup's return to Dundee in 1930. I am also grateful to the staff at Forfar Library and Wellgate Library in Dundee, who were always very helpful, as indeed were a plethora of football 'nuts' in Liverpool and elsewhere, who helped with the Everton years. Photographs came from the files of D.C. Thomson as well as from private sources. Ewan Malecki of Kirkcaldy drew the picture of Sunny Jim's encounter with Mrs Troup and her umbrella in 1914. A word of thanks to old friends of mine who gave me every encouragement - Richard Grant (and his wife Ann), David McGregor and David Patullo. Finally posthumous thanks to Colin McNab, John Jolly and my father Angus Potter, now dead for well over a decade and a half but who nevertheless talks to me about football and Forfar every day.

# INTRODUCTION

On February 24th 2002, Forfar Athletic met Rangers at Station Park in the Scottish Cup. The result was a humiliating, if predictable 0-6. As they said in Forfar, 'Six-nuthing, an we were even lucky tae get nuthing!' Rangers did not even have the decency to wait until the PA man had read out the teams before scoring their first goal! As the game was beamed live by BBC Scotland to the whole nation, the embarrassment was all the more acute.

Yet Forfar are a proud 'wee team', without whom the game would surely be so much the poorer. They have their moments ... and they do on occasion produce a truly great player. This book is a tribute to such a player.

It is now almost sixty years since Alec passed away, and the number of people who saw him in action must be very few indeed now. What a shame it would be if the name Alec Troup were allowed to pass into obscurity! This book is an attempt to keep his name alive, and to give youngsters a chance to appreciate what a great little man he was.

David W. Potter
Kirkcaldy
September 2010

# 1

# FORFAR: THE EARLY YEARS

Alexander Troup was born shortly after midnight on 12 May 1895 at 54 Queen Street, Forfar, Forfarshire (otherwise known as Angus), Scotland. The son of Benjamin and Christina Troup, he was the tenth child of the family. Already the Troups had seven sons and two daughters – William, Margaret, James, Nicoll, Benjamin, Joseph, David, Jane and John. In fact, Alec was the eleventh, for a child called George had died of whooping cough in 1876, at the age of one. It was a blow from which his mother, Christina, in particular, would not recover very easily.

In those pre-birth control and pre-welfare state times, it was by no means unusual to have families as large as this. There were, of course, no maternity hospitals in those days – unless you were very rich, in which case institutions called nursing homes came into play. If you were well enough off, you might have a doctor in attendance, otherwise a midwife would have to do the necessary. Sometimes for the very poor, not even a midwife would be there, and nature had to take its own course, although more often than not there would be a worldly-wise neighbour present who had seen it all before.

Not that the Troups were entirely poor. Although Benjamin had previously been a bleacher during the 1870s, from 1880 onwards he was described in the various birth certificates of his family as a fish merchant. This seems to have been a reasonably successful way of feeding his family. He would presumably go down to Arbroath, Dundee or Montrose with his horse and cart, buy a few loads of fish, and then sell them to the inhabitants of the inland Forfar or Kirriemuir. It was a tolerable living, and the Troups were definitely a financial degree or two above the impoverished factory workers who lived all around them. Yet Benjamin did not stay as a fish merchant forever. Other documents describe him as a general merchant or an iron merchant.

It was not an easy birth for Christina, in spite of her ample girth and general good health. She was now over forty and had undergone many births before, and Benjamin had his doubts about whether this was one birth too many for his seriously debilitated wife. In the event, things turned out well for Christina, although the baby was small and apparently very puny. Christina considered her youngest baby to be a particular blessing, and grew to be excessively (and sometimes overpoweringly) fond of little Alexander, but hated him being called 'Alec', 'Eck' or 'Sandy'.

Family life was good. The marriage had been a happy one since Chrissie McIntosh (in popular speech in the locality, a married woman would retain her maiden name)

*East High Street, Forfar, around the time of Troup's birth in 1895. On the right is St John's Episcopal church, where the Queen Mother worshipped as a young girl.*

*West High Street, Forfar, c. 1895.*

and Ben had tied the knot in Dundee in 1872, and they were much loved and respected in the town. Christina was originally from Kirriemuir, a small town five miles to the north of Forfar and soon to become famous for being the birthplace of J.M. Barrie, the creator of Peter Pan. (Incidentally, at the time of Alec's birth, Barrie was already making a name for himself in London.) Ben and Christina had met when they were both working in Dundee. Unlike most men of the time, Ben seems to have had no major weakness for the drink, and as a result, the family flourished. The family had previously lived at 170 East High Street, Petrie's Land, Backwynd, 120 East High Street, 16 Victoria Road and now enjoyed tolerably spacious premises in Queen Street.

The Forfar that Alec Troup was born into in 1895 was an interesting combination of things good and bad. The basic industry was jute. There were four or five factories – Moffat's, Don's, Craik's, Boath's and Lowson's – and they kept the town alive. Demand for jute had grown throughout the latter part of the nineteenth century with a great market in the United States of America. The winning of the Civil War by the Union in the North in 1865 had precipitated a tremendous drive westward in covered wagons. The wagons were covered in jute. Jute was also used for mailbags and carpet backing, and this was why Dundee and Forfar prospered.

But the prosperity was not always shared. Wages were low, and the factories were unhealthy, evil-smelling places. The work was not necessarily back-breakingly hard, but it was monotonous and dreary. Women could do the jobs, and as employers, always trying to find ways to pay their workers as little as possible, could get away with paying women less than men, there was more than occasionally seen the phenomenon of a working wife and an unemployed husband – although unemployment was not a widespread problem.

Contrary to the perceived vision of late Victorian Britain, society was not always stable, and in the jute industry, labour unrest was no isolated phenomenon. A story is told of how the Forfar jute owners were stoned by angry workers one night after returning from Dundee on the train, having failed to agree an increase in wages. The Forfar workers in the late nineteenth century were reasonably well organized under the leadership of one Tommy Roy, about whom songs were sung to the tune of the music hall hit 'Clementine': 'He's my darling, he's my darling, he's my darling Tommy Roy'. Sadly, such militancy evaporated when the said Tommy, the darling of the jute mills, absconded with the Union funds and somebody else's wife!

As already stated, unemployment was not the scourge in the 1890s that it would become in the 1930s, and the working classes were, generally speaking, in a slightly better state in Forfar than they would be in Dundee, for example, and certainly considerably better off than in the awful cities of Glasgow and Manchester. Being a small town, Forfar did not have as many appalling slum dwellings as Dundee did, and the very fact that there were fewer people around did indeed give everyone a chance, literally and metaphorically, to breathe.

There were also benefits to be had from living in a couthy Scottish town in late Victorian Britain. Education was firmly established in Forfar. The 1872 Education Act had, of course, made some sort of schooling compulsory throughout Scotland, but Forfar had had its Academy since at least 1819 and possibly earlier. By the middle of the nineteenth century, Forfar Academy had established itself as a fine place of learning, regularly sending 'lads o' pairts' (as intelligent young Scottish boys were called) to St Andrews University. Now, granted, those who went on to study Latin and Maths tended to be of middle class stock or from the farmers of the surrounding area, but most of the population had its grounding in the traditional three 'R's of Scottish education – reading, writing and arithmetic. Illiteracy was still a problem among some older people, but was being gradually and steadily eradicated.

Forfar was also lucky in that it was in the middle of the countryside, in the beautiful and fertile valley of Strathmore. It was thus a healthier place than most, and the town was also blessed by the munificence of one Peter Reid, manufacturer of children's sweets (particularly rock), who was a genuine philanthropist. This word 'philanthropist' is much overused, but it seems that Peter Reid was far more deserving of that name than the likes of Andrew Carnegie, for example, who was much vaunted in his home town of Dunfermline. Carnegie was quite clearly a grasping capitalist first, and a belated benefactor second. Carnegie's conversion to philanthropism and pseudo-Christianity only came once he realized that his conscience needed to be assuaged and his soul saved.

Not so Peter Reid. From the early days of his successful rock business he was a genuine lover of people, of children and of Forfar. His gift of a hall and a park are still very much a part of the town. He also had the couthy sense of good humour which characterises Forfarians even now. Children would go into his shop in Castle Street and ask for a 'but o' Peter Reid' (meaning a piece of Peter Reid rock). His reply was 'Certainly, lass, futten pairt o' me do you want?' Such a remark, if made out of context in the early twenty-first century, would, of course, have led to allegations and insinuations about paedophilia, but the humanitarian old Peter would have meant nothing by it, other than to give the children a laugh at his kindly humour. Peter died in 1895, the year of Alec's birth, but his influence remained.

In addition, Forfar was a community. The word 'community' is much devalued, but it means, according to the Latin derivation, a group of people with something in common. Forfar was certainly this. The disadvantage of such a community was that it could be small-minded and gossipy, but the benefit was that everyone rallied round those in adversity. When Alec was born into that large family in 1895, his mother would not have lacked support and help from her neighbours. A year later (in 1896) when Alec's eldest brother William married Jessie Dalgety in St James Church and the reception was held in the Masonic Hall, the whole town would turn out for an 'eyefull' or a 'gawp' at the beautiful bride and the Troups all in their finest clothes, including the babe-in-arms, young Alexander.

Nor was the Church so totally divorced from the working class in a small town as it was in the large cities. The Church persisted in having ridiculous, petty little feuds of its own with 'dissenters' and 'free' churches, but it was still respected. The workers were given the Sabbath (as Sunday was erroneously called) as their day of rest, and given the lack of any other entertainment on that day, attendance at church was practised by a large percentage of the population. The Church itself did nothing to dispel any apocalyptic rumours of what was to happen to anyone who did not attend, and the result was that Christianity did have some kind of a hold over the Forfar population.

However, it is clear that the influence of the Church was not total, for fornication and the resultant illegitimacies were common in almost every family, the Troups being no exception. In 1902, for example, James (another brother of Alec's) committed an indiscretion and had to do the decent thing and marry Jessie Shepherd. Birth control had not been heard of. Sad cases of domestic violence were reported in newspapers – women were battered, children were neglected, horses were ill-treated – and those who, almost a century later, wanted the return of Victorian values, frankly, did not know what they were talking about. It is often claimed that the Victorian era was an age of progress. So it probably was, but Heaven alone knows what life was like before!

The main problem as far as the working class was concerned was drink. In vain did the Church preach to its members and adherents the values of abstinence, and it would be no exaggeration to say that it was a very lucky household in Victorian Forfar that did not contain at least one person with a drink problem. The problem was that drink was comparatively cheap, it was certainly readily available and, frankly, there was very little else for anyone to do once they came out of the mind-numbingly dull jute factories. Mental or physical stimulation was difficult to find anywhere other than in the traditional 'sins' of sex and drink.

It was here that sport – in particular, football – came in. Forfar was luckier than most towns in that it had green areas set aside for recreational purposes. Cricket had been played in the town since soon after the Jacobite Rebellion of 1745. The game had been brought to Scotland by Hannoverian forces, and tended to be a middle-class pastime, played by the sons of gentlemen. The first mention of the famous Strathmore Cricket Club was in 1854, and describes them playing at a nearby Angus village called Kingoldrum. However, they soon moved into Forfar, playing at the Market Muir and the Steele Park before taking up residence in 1873 at their current ground near Forfar Loch– called Lochside – which is still one of the most beautiful cricket grounds in the country. Cricket became very popular among all classes of Forfar society (and still is), but towards the end of the century, it was football that the town went mad on.

Football developed slowly in Scotland. There was the famous dictum of James IV that 'Ye golfe and ye footieball should be utterly cryed doon'. Perhaps he deserved the fate that he met at Flodden in 1513! But there is no great evidence of football in Scotland until the middle of the nineteenth century when the game started to progress. Indeed, an anonymous Forfarian, writing in 1886, tells us of his childhood and attendance at the newly-built Forfar Academy in 1819. He says:

> The newly built academy was surrounded by a splendid park, which afforded ample space for the games we indulged in: marbles, handball, leaping and racing. We were also fond of shinty, which we played in Academy Street to the great annoyance of the passengers. But we had no game amongst us as that rude, vulgar and dangerous game called 'Football', neither did we have such dangerous things as a catapult. We were content with our tops and our piries.

In spite of the resistance of some sections of the middle classes, however, with increasing industrialisation and the coming of the railways which would facilitate travel, football simply took off in the latter part of the nineteenth century. The greatest stimulus to the game, which had hitherto been played by middle-class teams like Queen's Park (founded 1867) and Rangers (1873), was the fact that factories now closed at lunch-time on a Saturday. Perhaps the real significance of the founding of Celtic in 1887 (who played their first game in 1888) lay not so much in their contribution to the self-respect and self-esteem of the Irish in Scotland, as that the Celtic team were certainly a working-class organization. By the time that Alec Troup was born in 1895, there would be several football teams in the area – notably Forfar Athletic. Rumour had it that professionalism (legalised in 1893) had even spread to Forfar, and that the Athletic (having been in existence since 1884) actually paid some of their players for their Saturday afternoon's enjoyment!

Thus, as the young Alec grew up, he would no doubt frequently find himself playing, watching and talking about football. The location of his house in Forfar was a very short distance away from the East Bleaching Green – a fairly extensive piece of ground where clothes were dried and where football and other recreational activities could take place. Sometimes, of course, there would be no ball and a tin can had to do, but football would be played by all young boys for every hour of sunlight that the good Lord sent them. According to the Church, the good Lord did not like boys playing football on a Sunday, and although most mothers would make a reasonable attempt to stop their offspring from indulging in that game on that day, it was difficult to prevent it altogether.

Young Alec went to school at the turn of the century, probably in the first instance to the 'Spootie' School, at the junction of Castle Street and Queenswell Lane. School had been compulsory in Scotland for the last twenty-eight years, but in practice for a lot longer than that. The 1872 Education Act meant that the old parish system of education by the local church was done away with officially, but the Church still held a great deal of influence over the appointment of teachers, and there would have been no great debate about the ethos or culture of the school. Multiculturalism or pluralism was a long way off!

Education was avowedly and unashamedly Christian, and physical punishment in the shape of a leather strap was commonplace to persuade pupils of the benefits of the Christian lifestyle. This piece of leather, commonly known as the 'strap', the 'belt', the 'tawse' or the 'scud', was wielded with no little ferocity on children as young as five, in order to encourage habits of scholarliness and decency. It was, of course, in this respect a total failure, but many a teacher would solemnly tell her charges that she had two belts called Peter and Paul. Peter (however much it hurt Presbyterian Protestants to admit it) had been chosen as Christ's successor and Paul was the apostle who had spread Christianity throughout the Mediterranean Sea. Similarly, the two pieces of leather called Peter and Paul would 'spread' Christianity.

The doctrine of Christianity certainly encouraged the idea that Jesus was a gentle and loving man, but many pupils must have been perplexed at the contrast between the lifestyle of the Saviour who was 'meek and mild' 'loving' and 'kind' on the one hand, and the ferocious and terrifying demeanour of so many of his adherents. Eternal damnation was often threatened, both in church and in the classroom, for those who did not do as they were told. The word 'Hell' could be used, but only in the context of what happened to those who did not toe the line.

There was a sinister side to this brainwashing as well. The 'meek and mild' Jesus was held up as a role model for the purpose of encouraging youngsters to adopt a similar posture in their work places, and not to do subversive things like join trade unions or become members of the infant Labour party, which was threatening, apparently, to do so much to destroy Christian civilisation. Similarly, any young lady who chose to identify herself with the suffragette movement in their crusade for votes for women might well find herself called to one side after a church service one Sunday and told, quite categorically, that such activities were against God. It was also shameful that so much of the missionary work overseas was carried out in this paternalistic and patronising vein under the guise and masquerade of Christianity.

Thus, stories such as Jesus overturning the tables of the moneylenders in the temple would not have been given any great prominence – in fact, it would have been eschewed entirely – nor was the uncomfortable quote 'It is easier for a camel to pass through the eye of a needle than for a rich man to enter the Kingdom of Heaven' heard very often in the formative years of Alec Troup. Much more emphasis was laid on the need for 'self-respect' 'obedience' and 'gentleness'. Otherwise, the British Empire might not have been able to carry on its avowed task of 'civilising' the world.

It was the first winter of Alec's school career (a bad one, with lots of frost and snow) when late one night, a neighbour knocked on the door. His mother answered, and all Alec could hear were a few lowered voices as the family strained to hear what was being said. At last, Mrs Troup came through, and wiping a few tears from her eyes told the family that 'The Queen's awa'. This was 22 January 1901. It meant very little to Alec, of course, but he knew that she was called Victoria, and that Victoria Road in Forfar had been named after her, that she was old, and that his father and his older brothers had seen her once at Forfar station when she was on her way to stay at her castle at Balmoral.

The next day at school, the 'dominie' Mr Farquarson summoned everyone into one room and told them to wear something black for the next two or three days. The flag at the Town Hall was halfway up its pole, and nobody was allowed to laugh. Queen Victoria had been a great woman but was now at rest. Newspapers were full of hyperbole such as 'the saddest moment of our civilisation and history', although more objective historians would subsequently agree that things like the Black Death or the Crimean War had been a trifle more serious.

A happier occasion occurred a few months later, on 19 April 1901, when Alec's elder sister (Margaret) married one Robert Bell in St James church, followed by a reception in the Kirkton Hall. In those days, wedding receptions had a reputation of being riotous, rumbustious affairs, when even normally abstemious characters like the Troups would be permitted, nay even encouraged, to let their hair down. Weddings were also very friendly occasions, and the young Alec would have enjoyed telling his friends at the school about it.

As young Alec Troup went about the town in his first few years, he would have been aware of a few great 'seeings awa' (as the Forfar idiom went) of young men to fight for Queen (or King, after Queen Victoria's death) and Country in South Africa. Pipes would play, drums would beat, and women would cheer and wave flags as a gallant young Forfarian would be escorted along North Street with his kilt and kitbag to the station for the first leg of his journey to fight the Boers:

> Goodbye Dolly, I must leave you
> Though it breaks my heart to go
> Something tells me I am needed
> At the front to face the foe
> See the soldiers all are marching
> And I can no longer stay
> Hark! I hear the bugle calling,
> Goodbye, Dolly Gray!

The young man might or might not come back. If he did, he was a hero and treated like one – even more so if he came back injured. If he didn't return, then his grieving wife or weeping mother would be much comforted in church the following Sunday – then left to struggle on themselves. Nor would anyone have told the young Alec that this was a squalid little war, inflicted on the world by the British Empire's desire to steal diamonds from hitherto inoffensive Dutch farmers. Rather, much would be the talk of the heroism of people like Baden-Powell at places like Bloomfontein, Ladysmith and Mafeking.

As a youngster, a highlight in Alec's life would certainly have been the coronation of King Edward VII on 9 August 1902. It should have been earlier, but the King had an appendicitis attack and became one of the first to be operated upon for that condition. However, Edward recovered and the Coronation went ahead. Everybody had a flag to wave. Soldiers marched down East High Street, kilts swirling in the breeze, music was played, everyone had a day's holiday (with pay!), men got drunk, and children were given free sweeties and bars of chocolate with 'God Save the King' inscribed upon them. The young Alec may well have been mystified, however, as The Cross in Forfar did indeed contain many dignitaries, but no King. The King apparently was not to be in Forfar, as the actual Coronation was in London!

Another great event in the life of the young Forfarian was the opening of Shand's Picture Palace in around 1904. The moving pictures arrived in Forfar earlier than in most towns, when one David Shand opened a cinema in Roberts Street. It was very small (seating no more than about 100 initially, although by 1914 it was claimed to be the 'most comfortable place in Forfarshire'), but it was cheap and it showed all the latest films of the day. It was very primitive by our standards, but the young Alec would have been enthralled with the exploits of pirates and cowboys, brought from England and America by the man commonly known in Forfar as 'Shandie'.

*The Troup family photograph, taken around 1904. From left to right, back row: Benny, David, Nick, Will, James, Joe. Front row: Christina (mother), John, Meg, Ben (father), Jane. The youngest, Alec Troup, aged about nine, is seated in front.*

Forfarians have the habit of adding the letters 'ie' to the end of someone's name. It is often an affectionate diminutive – Alec would, of course, be called 'Troupie' – but more often it is merely a characteristic of the incredibly rich and idiosyncratic local dialect. Place becomes 'placie', face becomes 'facie', house becomes 'hoosie', and so on.

But even in these very early years, Alec thought about little other than football. He was bright enough at school, but no thought of higher education entered his or his family's minds. He would leave school in about 1910 at the age of fifteen and become apprenticed to a local plasterer. This was a good trade, and Alec was a conscientious young man who learned quickly. He could earn good money as a plasterer, they all said, but Alec would far rather earn money by playing football. In fact, the money would not have mattered...but fitba did!

Very early on in his life, it was noticed that he had a certain ability to control a football, beating the 'big leds' without much bother. He could dribble round his peers in Queen Street and when the other boys got fed up with him and his prowess, he would continue dribbling round the gas-lamp posts – or the 'lampies', as they were called. Forfar already had its football heroes. Alec was told all about Jimmy Dundas, who had gone from Forfar to play for Dundee at their famous ground at Carolina Port (before Dens Park was opened in 1899); and 'Ned' Doig, the goal-keeper of Sunderland at the time, who had played five times for Scotland, had been born at Letham, only five miles away. Rumour had it that Davitt McLean, the star man of Forfar Athletic, would sign for the mighty Glasgow Celtic.

Alec also followed the career of his brother. David, seven years older, was a fair player, and even managed several games for Forfar Athletic at senior level. But David soon found that his level was junior rather than senior, and he never turned professional. Yet he served as a good role model for Alec. Forfar Athletic – 'the Loons' – were considered to be Forfar's team, playing against the likes of Montrose, Arbroath, a host of Dundee teams, and even teams from as far afield as East Fife.

Alec would, of course, support his local team (and would continue to do so until he died) and in March 1906, a great thing happened to the town. For the first time ever, Forfar Athletic won the Forfarshire Cup. They did so at the neutral venue of Montrose, beating Arbroath, and although Alec, being less than ten years old, did not see the game, he remembered the team arriving back at the station with the band playing, everyone getting drunk and the sight of the silverware. Two years later, they won the Cup again, this time against Montrose at Dens Park, Dundee, and Alec was there. His brother Dave was in the team, and his father, no great football fan but very proud of his son, took Alec to see the game. It was a fine 4-1 victory for the Loons.

Alec also read in the papers about the great footballers of his day – about Celtic in Scotland, with their mighty men like Sunny Jim Young, Jimmy Quinn, Jimmy

*There does not appear to be a team picture of Forfar Athletic with Alec Troup. This one, however, contains his elder brother, Dave, who is pictured third from right in the second row. The trophy is the Forfarshire Cup, won in 1908. The author's great-uncle, George Potter, is one of the committee men, second from left in the back row.*

McMenemy; about the mighty Newcastle team in England; and about how Scotland played England every year. In 1906, Scotland beat England 2-1, and all of Forfar sang and danced with joy when somebody received the telegraph at the post office! A week or two later, a team called Everton won the English Cup, beating Newcastle 1-0. He knew where Newcastle was, but where was Everton? In Liverpool, somebody said. But the scorer of the only goal of the Cup Final (played at a place called the Crystal Palace in London) was a man called Sandy Young – and he was Scottish! Two of the others, John Sharp and Harry Makepeace (how everyone loved that unusual name!), also played cricket for Lancashire! What a team they must be, thought Alec in his childhood days.

April 1910 saw many significant things happening in Alec's life. On 2 April at Hampden Park, Scotland beat England 2-0 – and Alec was there. He went with older brother Dave and a few other boys, having saved up his pennies and eventually gained the reluctant permission of his mother and father. The crowd was huge, but Alec saw Jimmy McMenemy and Jimmy Quinn scoring the two goals which beat the English. Quinn, in particular, was an impresive figure – the bison with the broad shoulders:

> Didn't know Quinn?
> Pride of the Celtic?
> Look here, Saxon
> Where you bin?
> Not to know Quinn?
> Quinn of the Celtic?

The following week, if he had had more money, he might have gone again to Glasgow to see the Scottish Cup Final between Dundee and Clyde. Dundee were down and out until Forfar man Geordie Langlands saved the day and earned a replay. In fact, it needed a second replay before Sailor Hunter scored the winner and brought the Scottish Cup to Dundee for the first and (to date) only time. The whole area of Dundee and Forfar was lit up by this achievement, and great was the celebration – even on a Wednesday night. Symbolic of it all was the sight of the jute workers in Horsewater Wynd, Dundee – one of the worst slums in the city – dancing to the piper playing 'Bonnie Dundee' in an impromptu street party. Even the hardest-hearted of the jute barons would have smiled that night – and perhaps there was even some tolerance for those who did not quite make it in to work on time the next morning! Sadly, Dundee have never again since 1910 won the Scottish Cup, and there has been no need to resurrect the ghosts of Horsewater Wynd to dance again.

The 'middle' of the three Scottish Cup finals that year was played on a very stormy day. The storm had its significance in Forfar, for it almost blew the awning off Forfar's new entertainment centre which was opened that night. Fyfe and Fyfe – 'crème de la crème of vaudeville fare' – opened the pavilion (with seats for 800 people), which was located just off Castle Street. In later years, it would be called the 'Gaffie' and would be of a more substantial structure, but for the moment, the *Forfar Herald*'s prim journalist was delighted that the roof did not blow off.

> In some vaudeville shows, vulgarity is the keystone of success, but not so in Messrs Fyfe's pavilion. All nauseous efforts are rigorously eschewed, and the entertainment is fit for old and young. Cinematograph pictures, apart from the entertainment, bring the world within sight in a manner impossible to achieve other than by personal travel, and on account of their instructive value we recommend a visit to the Pavilion Electric Theatre. In conclusion, we need only say that the place is well lit by electricity, a special dynamo having been installed by Mr Fyfe for that purpose, and a much appreciated innovation is the arc lamp which shows the way out to Castle Street via Fonah Close.

No doubt Alec was there that night, and no doubt he was beginning to learn his job as a plasterer, but it was still football that really exercised the mind of the adolescent Alec. His own career was making a tentative beginning. Junior and juvenile football was played on a piece of land towards the north of the town called the Market Muir. Adjacent to the cattle market and over the railway line from Station Park, the home of Forfar Athletic, the Market Muir (or Markit Mair, according to the local vernacular) owed its name to the fact that cattle waiting to be sold were allowed to graze there. But there was a market or 'mert' only on Monday and Friday, and the rest of the time the grass was available for football. Several pitches were to be found there, and many games were played on a Saturday. There was also the Steele Park to the south of the town where West End played.

But it was Forfar Athletic who hit the national headlines on 11 February 1911. In their greatest result to date (and arguably their best ever) this humble, albeit ambitious, Northern League club were drawn against the mighty Falkirk (of the Scottish First Division) at Station Park – and beat them! Before a vast crowd of 2,000 – including 400 from Falkirk – the Loons won 2-0, goals coming from local boy James 'Jummer' Petrie and Brechin man David Easson. The scene was 'indescribable' says the *Forfar Dispatch*, and fifteen-year-old Alec Troup would have been one of the crowd acting 'as if they were in Bedlam – or Paradise'.

This result did indeed put Forfar on the map, and although the inevitable happened at Pittodrie in the next round (a 0-6 thumping from Aberdeen), Alec now had a taste of the joy of football. More importantly, the Forfar crowd now had expectations of success from their team. But Alec (or 'Alick', as his name was sometimes spelt) first had to serve his time in juvenile and then junior football.

There were four junior football teams in Forfar in the early years of the twentieth century. There was a North, East and a West End (apparently not a South End) and a Celtic, founded in conscious imitation of the great Glasgow institution which had done so much to popularise the game in Scotland. The Forfar teams played each other, of course, and occasionally ventured out of the Burgh on the train to play teams with lovely names like Ardendale, Dundee Harp, Arbroath Parkhead and Brechin Rangers. There is a quaint advertisement in the *Forfar Herald* for a game to be played at the Market Muir in 1912 between Celtic and Rangers. The only thing is that after the word Rangers it says, in brackets, Brechin. The Celtic, of course, is Forfar Celtic (was there another one?).

But before we come to the junior Grade, there was the juvenile. This was for even younger men than the juniors, and there was a great proliferation of such teams. There was a Fairfield, Celtic 'A' (more or less the reserves of Forfar Celtic) and a team called Aston Villa. Also, every town seemed to have a football team called Victoria, in honour of the late Queen. Alec often wondered why there was so much fuss about her. She had lived in London, and in any case had now been dead for a few years. People like Jimmy Quinn, who scored a hat-trick in the 1904 Scottish Cup Final and, of course, the goal that finally beat England in 1910, was a far more interesting person.

Alec, being very small, tended to be rejected by teams as they thought he was quite likely to be pushed out of the game, but he persisted, turning up every night for practice and showing a tremendous appetite for the game and eventually, around 1912, Celtic 'A' gave him a chance in the Forfar Juvenile League. Very soon, it was seen that he had a tremendous ball control as well as the ability to dribble and to cross a ball. Not least of his many skills was his turn of pace, through which he was able to avoid the desperate lunges of defenders and thus escape serious injury.

The junior team North End also kept an eye on him, and throughout the early months of 1913, his name is mentioned now and again in the *Forfar Herald*, whose reporter 'Rambler' had an 'Among the Juniors' column. Troup appears to have managed to gain selection for the occasional game – on 15 March he played in the black-and-gold stripes of North End when they lost 1-3 to the Maroons of East End, but he is mainly mentioned playing for the juveniles of Celtic 'A'. On 12 April, Troupe (sic) scored twice for the 'Bhoys' (sic) as they beat Aston Villa 3-2. North End now thought he was worth another game for them, and the following week Alec scored, as North End beat Arbroath Fairfield 4-3, sending the 'Round O' men back home unhappy. (The Round O is a reference to Arbroath Abbey.)

These were heady days for North End – they won the Forfar & District League and the Forfar & District Cup, as well as reaching the semi-final of the Forfarshire Junior Cup which contained the Dundee teams. These games appear to have been keenly contested and to have aroused quite a lot of passion – occasionally of the wrong sort. For example, on 28 April 1913, a Monday Holiday or the 'Fast' as it was locally known, in spite of a day of foul weather, a 'goodly turnout of spectators' were watching a game between North End and Celtic (in which Troup does not seem to have been involved) when a player called Byars (it is not clear for which team he played) was 'struck' (it is similarly unclear whether by an opponent or a spectator) and a free fight developed. Order was restored, but it seems that some of the 'goodly' turnout had consumed a goodly amount of alcohol. On another occasion, the club linesman of East End (whose anonymity is protected by the *Forfar Herald*) struck a referee.

Before the new season of 1913/14 began, there was the big event of the summer calendar – the Forfar Games. Held at the Steele Park on the Monday of the Forfar Holiday week at the end of July, they attracted competitors from far and wide for caber-tossing, athletics races, wrestling, pillow-fighting and dancing contests. Visitors from Dundee, Aberdeen and Perth would throng the town, and the weather was predictably glorious. Stories would be told of the two Forfarians lost in the Sahara Desert where they had been vainly prospecting for gold, crawling on their hands and knees with the relentless sun beating down on them. When one told the other that it was 27 July, the other one said 'They're gettin a bra' day for the Farfar Games, min!'

The highlight was the five-a-side football tournament. North End fielded Troup (although he was technically still a Forfar Celtic signing) for this prestigious event and delighted their fans by winning it, beating another North End (of Dundee) in the final by two goals to nil. On 1 August 1913, the eve of the new season, North End announced that they had signed Alec Troupe (sic) from Celtic. There was possibly a 'signing-on' fee involved, maybe as much as £5, but he had not yet reached the professional level.

Thus Alec donned officially the black-and-gold stripes of Forfar North End for the 1913/14 season, as distinct from the previous season when he had been a trialist. He was usually played at inside left, but occasionally we find him at left half. He does not seem to have appeared on the left wing, although on several occasions he took corners from which goals were scored. What little is said about him in the *Forfar Herald* is consistently good, although the club suffered a major disappointment when they lost to Ardenlea of Arbroath at Gayfield in the Forfarshire Junior Cup on 8 November, where the receipts were '£8, and possibly a bit more'.

However, it was possibly the rave notice of 13 December – 'Troup, though usually in the forward line, was the shining light of a good half-back line' – after a game against Dundee Stobswell that was to change his life.

# 2

# THE EMERGING GENIUS

Alec was sitting having his tea one night between Christmas and New Year after a hard day's work at his plastering, when there was a knock at the door of his Queen Street house. 'There's a man here to see you, Alexander', said his mother. It was James Black, secretary of Forfar Athletic. Mr Black explained the situation. Davie McLean, who had briefly re-joined Forfar having played for Celtic, Sheffield Wednesday and famously for Scotland in April 1912 at Hampden Park (when he helped Scotland to a 1-1 draw against England), was off back to Sheffield, having made his peace with his former employers in the Steel City. McLean, of course, was the only Forfarian to date who had won a Scottish cap. Little could Black have realised, as he looked upon this tiny, young, fair-haired, earnest eighteen year old, that he was looking at the next. Black's idea to plug the gap (McLean would have been unavailable in any case, for he was ill with 'flu) was to put Geordie Langlands in McLean's place at centre, and bring in Troup at inside left to replace Geordie. One of Black's committee men had been watching the juniors and was very impressed by the young Troup.

It was McLean's Celtic career that had caused the greatest stir in local legend. In particular, it was his role in the League-winning Celtic team of 1909 that had impressed everyone. Celtic played eight games between 19 April 1909 and 30 April of that year in order to win the League and pip Rangers and Dundee. McLean played in six of them and scored six goals. He might have gone on to become a Celtic legend, but was unfortunate in that he played at the same time as Jimmy Quinn. Also, he did not get on at all well with the famous Celtic manager Willie Maley, whose occasionally bullying methods of man-management did not always endear him to the young Forfarian. McLean's nominal Protestantism may also have hindered his Celtic ambitions at that time, although most historians would agree that Quinn was the better player.

McLean was thus, even in his early days, a soldier of fortune. An individualist, quixotic, stubborn, occasionally headstrong and no great toady to dictators, McLean was deservedly a local hero, in spite of (or perhaps because of) his acerbic nature. He kept falling in and out with Black and Forfar Athletic, for whom he actually signed four times in his lengthy career!

The *Forfar Herald* of late December 1913 laments the departure of McLean. 'His boomerangs will be much missed' at Station Park, says the scribe, who is perhaps not as well versed in aboriginal culture as he could be, for boomerangs, one would imagine, might come back to hit him in the face! But he wishes McLean well at Owlerton (the previous name for Hillsborough), before making the mistake of saying that he will do well for the Blades. The Blades are, of course, Sheffield United, who played at Bramall Lane. Wednesday's nickname is The Owls, and they were so called because of the name of their ground.

When Alec Troup was called up by Forfar's secretary, James Black, it would appear that he was being called upon to be McLean's successor. This was a mighty calling. Troup's debut for Forfar Athletic was on New Year's Day 1914 in the Central League. By tradition, there was a local Angus derby against Arbroath on that day, and Troup was included at inside left. It must have been a great day for his family to see him take the field in the black-and-blue stripes of Forfar. Elder brother Dave had also, of course, worn the colours, but without any great success. Now here was another Troup representing his town.

Arbroath wore their colours of maroon to symbolise the famous lighthouse there. In fact, their nickname was 'the Red Lichties'. Forfar's reason for wearing blue and black is not so obvious. Their nickname was 'the Loons' – a 'loon' in Angus being a young man, not, as in other parts of the United Kingdom, a shortened form for the word lunatic.

There was, and still remains, a healthy rivalry between the two towns, Forfar and Arbroath. Communications between the two had been frequent since the opening of the railway on 3 January 1839 (one of the first in Scotland). Forfar was the county town. The county was still called Forfarshire, much to the chagrin of the Red Lichties, whose town was considerably larger. Arbroath was a great fishing port, specialising in 'smokies', and people like Ben Troup made his living from buying fish in Arbroath and selling them in Forfar.

Of all days to make a debut, New Year's Day was the greatest in Forfar's calendar. It was a fixture which attracted a large crowd, even including people who would not normally have attended a football match. The recent frost had thawed and the pitch would be soft. Train after train of Arbroath people rolled into the station, a mere 100 yards from the ground (hence its name of Station Park). New Year's Day being one of the few holidays that the working man got, the town had talked about little else for weeks beforehand. Christmas passed almost unnoticed in Scotland in 1913 – it was New Year that was the big day. Drink would be consumed in great quantities and the revelry for the previous fourteen hours before the kick off would have been intense.

The teams were:
Forfar Athletic: G. Scott; Ferguson and C. Scott; Bruce, Chapman and Leighton; Mitchell, Walker, Langlands, Troup and Petrie.
Arbroath: Crumley; McKenzie and Peters; Dinnie, Taylor and Brown; Herron, Guild, Milne, Thomson and Ritchie.

The dressing room was not in the stand in those days. It was a stone-built house (commonly referred to as the 'hoosie') located behind the east goal. Players would come out of the 'hoosie' and run through the crowd (some 4,000 that day) to take the field. The Arbroath supporters would laugh at the debutant (5ft 5in and 10 stone 7 pounds) who looked just like a wee boy among such big men as Langlands and Chapman. His Forfar Athletic jersey was perforce a couple of sizes too big, and one loudmouth described him with a touch of hyperbole as looking like 'a sheep lost in the Grampians'. But the jeers were silenced as Troup dribbled and teased, taunted and tantalised the big Arbroath defenders and inspired Forfar to a 6-1 win, scoring twice, although one goal was a deflection.

Forfarians had seldom seen anything like this. This was football at its inspirational best. Forfar being the place it was, questions like 'Fa's that wee led at inside left?' were soon answered by 'That's Ben Troup's young led – ye ken 'im, he bides in Queen Street, he's mither's a McIntosh, they've got 'im fae North End. Ye mind o' his brither Dave – thus ane's meant tae be better', and the crowd left singing the praises of 'wee Eckie'. Ben Troup himself, although no great football fan, sat proudly in the stand with his sons David and Benny that day, and had his hand shaken by exultant Forfarians as well as sporting Arbroath supporters (some of his business connections), who wished him a Happy New Year. Forfar's secretary James Black (or 'Jeem', as he was commonly referred to) congratulated himself on a new find. We might be able to make 'a shullin or twa' on him, he mused, in his typically mercenary fashion.

The *Forfar Dispatch* the following Thursday enthused about ' ... the youngster Troup, whose wizard-like footwork and mature judgement more than made up for his lack of pounds and inches'. The *Forfar Herald* agrees, albeit more mundanely: 'Troup showed an ability which justified his inclusion' and 'the inside trio made a really good combination'. More was to come. Troup was similarly inspired in the next game against Bo'ness on Saturday 3 January. The reporter of the *Dispatch* was apprehensive when he saw the Bo'ness team come out. They were 'buirdly chiels beside whom the homesters looked little bookit', meaning (for those not well versed in Angus dialect) that the Bo'ness fellows were burly individuals in contrast to the lesser build of the Forfarians. Not that it mattered. Forfar won again, and the inside trio of Walker, Langlands and Troup were brilliant.

As the crowd departed in the gloom of those early January afternoons to nurse hangovers or consume more alcohol, there was much talk about these great Forfar performances. It was just as well, as handshakes were exchanged to wish everyone all the best in 1914, that no one really knew exactly what that fateful year would bring – nor could anyone have predicted that a sizeable percentage of the crowd would celebrate their next New Year at places far removed from Forfar or Arbroath.

In the *Forfar Herald*, the writer who called himself 'The Loon' was enthusiastic. 'Forfar has got the football fever again. In factories, pubs and street corners, there is talk of little else. There was a reference to it in a local pulpit last Sunday, and they even discussed it at the town council'. The *Dispatch* clearly knew as little about what was to happen in Europe that year as anyone else did, and was far more worried about the possible transfer of Geordie 'Purkie' Langlands. Geordie was, of course, the man who rescued Dundee in the Scottish Cup Final of 1910 with a late equaliser, but he had now returned to Forfar. Rumours were by now abounding, however, that Notts County were interested in him and he might be on his travels once again. Having lost McLean, Forfar didn't want to lose Langlands as well.

But, even if that were to happen (it didn't, in the event) the *Dispatch* was so confident about the way that Forfar were playing (given the potential of young Troup) that it reminded its readers about a 'cinematograph film' that had been shown at the Reid Hall last winter, in which a frog had been shown with its brain removed 'yet the creature kicked as vigorously as before'.

Forfar were certainly kicking vigorously. Vigorously enough to earn themselves a visit in February from the mighty Glasgow Celtic on Scottish Cup business. Forfar's first-ever brush with the big-time came with the news in early February that if Forfar beat East Stirlingshire in the Scottish Cup, Celtic would come to town – Celtic, *the* Glasgow Celtic, the mighty Celts, the bould Celts, still in 1914 happy to be called 'the Irishmen'. Celtic were the team which had transformed Scottish football since their foundation little more than quarter of a century earlier.

Merchiston Park, Bainsford, near Falkirk, the home of East Stirlingshire, thus saw an invasion of Forfarians on 7 February to see the cup tie to earn the winners the right to entertain such distinguished visitors. Attracted by a cheap rate football special (3s for adults and 1s 6d for children), over 300 people from the town gave an affirmative answer to the question on everyone's lips 'Are ye gaein tae Falkirk on Saturday?'. 'The Loon' in the *Forfar Herald* is snobbish enough to note approvingly that the crowd contained some magistrates, at least one doctor and at least one lawyer among them. He is also very impressed by the banner, which was unfurled in club colours and read:

> Play up the Loons
> Win, Lose or Draw,
> You Are The Best Team
> Of the Twa

Inspirational stuff, that! Much was the talk on the train about little Eckie Troup. Both Forfar papers (and indeed the *Dundee Courier*) had been ecstatic about him since his debut at the New Year. 'Clever footwork', 'smart touches', 'rare judgement', 'difficult to surpass in provincial football' and 'guid gear comes in sma' buik' were among the quotes about 'wee Eck' or the 'boy wonder'. Occasionally, someone would worry about whether he had come too far too soon, but there was no sign of that. He was outstanding that day at East Stirling, but must have been heartbroken to see the home team earn a replay through a penalty, which the Forfar papers (hardly surprisingly) categorised as 'soft' and 'doubtful'.

Forfar duly beat East Stirling 2-0 in the replay on 14 February at Station Park. 'The Loon' was ecstatic:

> The boy forward was in sparkling humour. He dodged and doubled to
> some purpose and his passes were marked with rare accuracy. There was
> not a better forward on the park than Eck. He did however miss a chance
> and no wonder he scratched his head – for it was an easy one!

The town now took a collective intake of breath for the following Saturday. Arguments about the Suffragettes, poverty, Ireland and that crazy Kaiser man took a back seat in local hostelries like Jarman's and the Salutation Hotel in favour of how

'Wee Troupie' (as he was already affectionately called) would get on against the mighty men. The refined ladies of the Women's Guild at the Old Kirk were even moved to discuss this mighty event, and some of them (those with an indulgent husband or father who could protect them) were on Saturday going to see their first-ever football match. What a pity that Davitt McLean had returned to Sheffield Wednesday. He would have 'rumbled them up' – a delightfully vague Forfar phrase which seems to combine 'throw the defence into confusion' with 'shoulder-charge the goalkeeper'! McLean always was a better player than Quinn! What about this Patsy Gallacher the Celtic supporters all talked about? Naw, 'Lichton' (Leighton to those not of these parts) would 'sort him oot'. Forfar would do it, 'for they are on £5 a man to win' averred someone who clearly had inside information denied to lesser people. 'We bate Falkirk yon time, we'll beat Celtic this year'.

In truth, this was sheer moonshine and unrealistic optimism. Forfar were not yet even in the Scottish League and would not be admitted until well after the First World War. The game ended 0-5 for the illustrious visitors, and they won themselves many friends by their fine play and their courteous demeanour. However, the scribe in the *Forfar Dispatch* was less than totally enamoured with the Glasgow visitors. He had clearly been paying attention to his Old Testament in church the previous Sunday, for he makes frequent mention of 'David' and 'Goliath'. Not only that, but there seems to have been a Philistine element in Celtic's play as well, he adds darkly. The *Forfar Herald* concurred and singled out Young and McMaster for criticism, Young in particular for his fouling of Troup, but 'the ease with which the laddie beat his redoubtable opponents was diverting'. The play of Patsy Gallacher, however, for Celtic was similarly 'scintillating'.

One or two things happened which were bizarre. The mighty Jimmy Quinn, now injury-prone and not playing that day, was seen to carry the hamper containing the kit off the train while smoking a clay pipe and looking for all the world 'just like an ordinary man'. And what a bunch of ragamuffins came off the train with them! Men with scarred faces, women with painted ones and one or two children who wore thick stockings – but no shoes! These were the tribe happy to be called 'The Glasgow Irish'.

In contrast to the palpable penury of their adherents, Celtic made the surprisingly snobbish decision to change for the game at the recently opened baths and then be ferried by charabanc (a primitive form of bus) to Station Park. This was in order to avoid the admittedly sub-standard accommodation of 'the hoosie'. While Celtic were changing at the baths, Jock Airth, the baths manager, overheard Celtic manager Willie Maley telling them all to 'watch that young fellow called Troup'.

Well, 'Sunny Jim' Young, Celtic's captain, certainly did that. Sunny was, of course, a Scottish international and with his blond hair was instantly recognisable. He enjoyed earning the wrath of opposition crowds by winding them up. Several times, Eckie Troup was downed by Sunny, who instantly faked innocence and picked up the shaken young Forfarian, apologising to the referee and Forfar's secretary Jim Black, who was acting as club linesman that day. It was presumably this that the *Forfar Dispatch* saw, subliminally and allegorically, as the David *v*. Goliath element in the game.

The crowd did see enough to show them that Troup was getting the better of the

*An artist's impression of the infamous incident in February 1914 at Forfar, when Alec's mother belted Celtic's famous Scottish internationalist 'Sunny Jim' Young with her umbrella for repeatedly fouling Alec.*

mighty Sunny Jim. He dribbled and teased his way past Young to the delight of the local crowd and the admiration of the Glasgow supporters, but the story that he put the ball past Sunny's legs, then dived between them to get the ball at the other side would appear to owe a little to rhetorical exaggeration. Sunny was annoyed at all this, because no one, up till now, had made a fool of him. He was indeed prodigal with fouls, even at a stage of the game when Celtic had the game well won, and was given a lecture or two by the referee, Mr W. Shanks of Falkirk. 'Young was given a stern finger wigging or two by the magisterial Mr Shanks' says the *Forfar Herald*, but no further action was taken.

However, a certain amount of divine retribution was to come Sunny's way. He did not fool Eckie's mother. At full time, as the triumphant Celtic team made for their charabanc, the crowd gathered round for a view of these demi-gods. Christina Troup was less impressed. Like a mother hen on the trail of someone who had injured her brood, she leaned forward and made to hit Sunny over the head with her umbrella. 'Tak that, you durty Glesca bugger!' she screamed, but fortunately such maternal soccer hooliganism was restrained by calmer elements, including her own husband, Ben Troup, who was presumably somewhat embarrassed at this.

In these days there were no neutral linesmen. Each club provided one, and there was a code of honour (not always strictly observed) that the linesman did not cheat. In this case managers Willie Maley and Jim Black did the needful. Black was, in fact, very experienced at this job. He had been a referee (his distinctions including officiating at the first-ever game at Dens Park, Dundee in 1899) and had also been Scotland's linesman in the international against England in 1912. Towards the end of the game, he missed an obvious 'fling' (as throw-ins were then known) for Forfar. His enemies (and he had many) turned on him and 'Jeem' offered an unusual plea – 'Sorry, leds, ah wisna peying attention. Ah couldna tak ma een aff they twa leds ower there' pointing his flag at Celtic's prodigiously talented Patsy Gallacher and Forfar's brilliant young Alec Troup.

Both teams had their tea at the Queen's Hotel that night. The Queen's was then owned by the famous cyclist John Killacky, one-time world champion and a good friend of both Willie Maley and Jim Black. Maley was, as always, charming and encouraging, and predicted a great future for young Alec Troup, and the great Jimmy McMenemy, commonly known as 'Napoleon', was also gracious to Forfar and in particular to Troup. The referee Mr Shanks was apparently impressed as well and was quoted as saying that he thought that Troup was a 'prospect'.

Someone from the Celtic party ventured his opinion that Troup was good, but that perhaps his lack of inches would prevent any further progress than rural Forfar. Mr Black overheard that remark and exploded 'What? The wee led's a futba' artist fae the croon of his heid to the tips of his taes! He's as neat as ninepence, can trap a ba', beat a man, syne … ' Mr Black was not normally guilty of laying it on thick about his players, otherwise they might get too big-headed and even ask for more money, but on this occasion he did not hold back, extolling the virtues of his new-found genius.

After the meal and before Celtic boarded the train to take them back to Glasgow, Alec made a deliberate point of seeking out and talking to the great Patsy Gallacher. Both were men of small stature and slight build – but both were to become masters of the game. They talked at length about the problems of being so small, smiled and joked with each other and departed on the best of terms. Their paths would cross again on several occasions in the future.

The teams on that great day in Forfar's history were:

Forfar Athletic: J.Scott: Ferguson and C.Scott: Bruce, Chapman and Leighton; Easson, Walker, Langlands, Troup and Petrie.
Celtic: Shaw; McNair and McGregor; Young, Johnstone and Dodds; McAtee, Gallacher, McColl, McMenemy and Browning.

This game was the game in which Troup won his spurs. He would remember it, and be remembered for it. Of all people to watch a game involving Celtic, William Wilton, the manager of Rangers, was the most distinguished. In circumstances which it would be hard to parallel to-day, Wilton attended the meal at the Queen's Hotel and then travelled back to Glasgow with the Celtic party! He must have been impressed by Troup, but it was Forfar's left back, Chick Scott, that he signed. Chick was a fine player, but his playing career with Rangers never really got started before he was tragically killed in the First World War.

Celtic would win the League and Cup double that season, but it was back to the Central League for Forfar and the mundane business of collecting League points for the rest of the season. Kirkcaldy United are one of the many 'ghost' teams of Scottish football. One thinks of St Bernard's, who never survived the Second World War, Third Lanark who went to the wall in 1967 and a few others. Kirkcaldy United did not survive the First World War. The reasons were a high casualty rate among their players, the loss of their ground for war purposes and a sad inability to keep pace with Kirkcaldy's other team – Raith Rovers.

In 1914, the ultimate goal for teams like Kirkcaldy United and Forfar Athletic was membership of the Scottish League. Both teams had been unsuccessful in that respect so far, and were currently playing in the Central League. By March of that year, it was obvious that both teams were going to end up respectably placed, but neither of them were likely to win it.

As Forfar travelled to Kirkcaldy in the train that day, James Black, holding court as normal to the other officials (and anyone else within earshot) enthused about his new teenage star, Alec Troup. He was small and thin, but so too was Patsy Gallacher of Celtic, and both of them had wonderful ball control, and the ability to pass a ball. More than that, Troup was speedy and perhaps the most important of all, he had a brain for the game. He could spot the weaknesses in the opposition's defence and exploit them. 'In fact,' pontificated James to all and sundry on the train, 'I wad say that Troopie has mair gaein for him than Gallacher, judgin bi whit we sa at Station Park'.

Kirkcaldy United played at Scott's Park in the eastern part of Kirkcaldy, quite close to Sinclairtown station, so the team could walk there. Young Troup, being the youngest, had the job of carrying the hamper along with some other youth. The weather was bright enough, although there had been quite a lot of recent rain and the ground was heavy. The referee, Mr Munro of Musselburgh, however, had no problem in allowing the game to go ahead as long as one of the goalmouths was heavily sanded. The pitch was on a slope, unfortunately, and water tended to flow towards one end.

This game was the benefit match for goalkeeper Jim Dorward who had been with Kirkcaldy United since 1901 and claimed to be their first-ever professional player. This meant that a collection was taken for him at half time, and he was given his own special cheer at the start.

It was Kirkcaldy who scored first when McAleer, a trialist from Bathgate, took advantage of hesitancy in the Forfar defence. But Forfar were playing with the advantage of the slope, and Kirkcaldy's defence were having a great deal of difficulty in coping with the wiles of wee Troup, who was so elusive in spite of the heavy ground. Before half time, Forfar had equalised, and it was a tragedy for Dorward, the beneficiary. Troup had beaten a man on the edge of the box and shot with a power surprising for such a slight youth. Dorward got his hands to the ball, but it was wet and heavy and he could not hold it. Geordie Langlands was on hand to tap it home.

Coming just before his half time collection, this was a bad moment for Dorward but his spirits were improved when left winger Black restored Kirkcaldy's lead just as Mr Munro was about to point to the pavilion for half time.

The second half saw the game continuing at ferocious pace, although by now the pitch was cutting up badly. Forfar equalised following some fine work by left winger Petrie, who crossed the ball to Langlands to hammer it past Dorward. A winner could have come at either end, but it was Kirkcaldy who won it. With the advantage of playing down the slope, McAleer won a ball on the edge of the box and 'carried well in' as the *Fife Free Press* put it. This means he dribbled past several Forfar players and walked the ball into the net.

It was a fine game, although disappointing for Forfar in what turned out to be their last-ever visit to Scott's Park, Kirkcaldy. It would nevertheless be recalled by one aged Kirkcaldy man who, even as late as 1993 and virtually on his deathbed, would regale his visitors with stories about a wee Forfar lad called Troup.

Kirkcaldy United: Dorward, Cairns and MacDonald; Wilkie, Whyte and Fotheringham; Fisher, Anderson, McAleer, Gourlay and Black.
Forfar: Scott; E. Ferguson and D. Ferguson; Nicol, Chapman and Leighton; Adamson, Walker, Langlands, Troup and Petrie.

The rest of the season saw Forfar playing well enough in the Central League without ever threatening to win it. They beat the likes of Arbroath and Stenhousemuir but lost to Lochgelly. Troup was now such a favourite of 'The Loon' in the *Forfar Herald* that he was simply called 'Eck', 'Eckie' or the 'little chap'. The last game of the season was lost to Armadale – and the *Forfar Dispatch* uses a Scottish word called 'disjaskit' to describe them. It means tired and exhausted, as indeed they were at the end of a long season. The club applied for membership of the Scottish League Second Division and, although they now had the backing of Celtic, whom they had clearly impressed in February, they failed narrowly in their bid.

It would be the Central League (as well as a curious institution calling itself the Northern League, which tended to consist of Dundee and Aberdeen's reserve teams) yet again for the 1914/15 season, but hopes were high. At the AGM in the Masonic Hall on 12 May, Black painted a rosy picture of financial stability and a good football team. With young Troup, anything seemed possible – although by now both Dundee and Aberdeen were interested. Forfar, however, were not keen on doing any business yet.

Nor was Troup himself keen on any sort of move. Falkirk's schoolteacher inside left James Croal, thrice capped for Scotland, had been transferred to Chelsea in April 1914 and the Bairns saw Troup as a replacement. Twice an offer was made, but Black knocked them back. Troup was keen to serve out his time as a plasterer in any case, and was not yet ready for full-time football. Besides he was a Forfar boy who loved his home town.

Yet he was now near the end of his apprenticeship with William Milne of Wellbraehead, and the thought of turning to professional football must have entered his head. But he was still not yet in his twenties, and there was time enough. He trained hard for the coming season, tried to put on weight and gain height, but found both of these objectives very difficult. He played a little cricket, had a swim or two at the lovely new baths, ran a few sprints over 100 yards and generally enjoyed the glorious summer of 1914. He may well have gone to see the opera *Maritana* put on by the local group, or he could have enjoyed the film *Antony and Cleopatra* at Shand's Picture Palace.

Meanwhile, although football was idle, Forfar's energetic secretary James Black was 'searching the world like Diogenes with his lantern' (according to the erudite *Forfar Dispatch*) for talent for the new season and managed to dig up Bannerman and Scrymgeour from Dundee. There was every reason to feel optimistic, thought Black. We clearly have something in 'Wee Troupie' and Geordie Langlands had turned down the offer from Notts County and was content to play for his local team. Surely we could win the Central League this year and then get into the Scottish League?

Elsewhere in the town that summer, the weather was glorious. A new church was opened in the east of the town called the Lowson Memorial, with Revd P.G. Millar being called as the first minister. Cricket was in full swing with Strathmore doing well. Another team called St John's (based in the local Episcopalian church, where a local lady called Elizabeth Bowes-Lyon of Glamis Castle had recently been confirmed) played at St Margaret's Park and were holding their own against the Second XIs of Montrose and Brechin. At Forfar Academy, the main prize of the year, the Latin Medal, was won by one Howard Marshall – this was mentioned in the same edition of the *Forfar Herald* which carried towards the back page the news of an assassination of one of the Austro-Hungarian royal family in Sarajevo, Serbia.

The outside world was of no great interest to Forfarians. The assassination of some Austrian archduke in central Europe at the end of June did not appear to be of any great relevance. It was only as the intense heat of July continued that phrases such as 'European situation' gave way to 'crisis' then 'grave situation' then 'emergency'. Then the conversation turned to politics, as the Kaiser of Germany seemed to be meddling with all sorts of things that were of no concern to him. He wouldn't plunge the world into war, would he? He was, after all, the grandson of Queen Victoria and the cousin of King George V. At the time, many were distrustful of the Germans, wary of the large empire they had built up, but they were certainly not considered enemies.

The amazing thing about it all was its suddenness. Towards the end of July, Austria-Hungary, the Kaiser's allies, attacked Serbia as a result of the assassination that had occured a month earlier. The Serbs appealed for help to their fellow Slavs in Russia. Russia got involved and brought in France, with whom they had an alliance. Germany then came in on the side of the Austro-Hungarians. Britain was not yet involved, but the Kaiser committed the fateful step of allowing himself to be persuaded by his generals to attack France through Belgium, with whom Britain had signed a neutrality treaty in 1839. Had he not agreed to this in the hope of landing a quick knock-out blow on France, the British Empire might have stayed neutral in 1914, and a smaller, less horrific war might well have been the result.

The story went that the Kaiser repented of his decision to invade Belgium, but too late. The trains were already speeding towards Belgium and could not be stopped – the country was already being invaded. Britain now had to get involved. Small nations had to be protected from big bullies – that is, if the bullies were not the British Empire itself!

But this mad turn of events, in a perverse way, meant that there was something to get excited about. One must never forget the sheer boredom of life and work in these jute factories. There was now a chance to do something different. It was therefore a happy atmosphere at Station Park, Forfar on 29 August 1914, as one would have expected for the first home game of a new season. It was Forfar's second season in the Central

League, and as it was a fine day, it looked as if well over 2,000 people had paid their 4d for the game, including around a hundred or so who had come inland from Montrose to support that day's opponents.

But there was added reason for euphoria. It was this thing called war, which added a frisson of excitement to the local population. A few weeks before, when war was declared on 4 August, the flags had been out and the band had been playing as the first detachment of the Territorials had marched from the Drill Hall in the New Road to the station to join the British Expeditionary Force. Others were keen to join them. It would be a shame not to, for 'it would all be over by Christmas'. (An even more optimistic German officer said 'before the leaves fall'). The temptation to get away from those boring monotonous jute factories, even for a brief spell, was enticing. Already, it was said, the British Army was in the field and fighting against the Germans.

The *Dispatch* carried an appeal from Sergeant Osler at the Drill Hall for recruits. The cinemas – Shand's Picture Palace in Roberts Street ('Where Everybody Goes', according to their advertising slogan) and The Pavilion in Castle Street were both showing two war films from the Boer War called *The Two Sergeants* and *A Deal with the Devil*, and jokes and cartoons were even printed in the 'paperie' (as the *Forfar Dispatch* styled itself) about Scottish soldiers in kilts – 'I'm neither cauld wi ma kilt, nor kilt wi the cauld' said a man, clearly wearing a pair of thick pants underneath.

But it was a great game of football at Station Park that day which Forfar won 6-3. Montrose scored twice, which 'plunged the crowd into melancholy', but then Forfar ran riot and scored five before half time. The architect of this was indeed Troup who, in spite of several hefty challenges from Montrose defenders about twice his height and bulk, simply kept running, dribbling and feeding the other forwards. Langlands scored a hat-trick, then Walker and then Petrie had the Montrose defence reeling and the Forfar crowd cheering.

At half time the players went off as normal, but before the second half started, the players lined up on the touchline as two figures appeared. One was instantly recognised as James Black the manager, secretary or general 'heid led' of Forfar Athletic, but the other was a tall, well-built man in military uniform complete with Black Watch tartan. 'Blackie' asked for silence and got it instantly (he didn't always, for it was not unknown for him to be booed) and introduced Sergeant Osler to the crowd. The sergeant talked about the Empire and the King, what the Germans were doing in Belgium, the good pay in the Army, and he urged all young men below the age of forty to sign up.

He was given a polite round of applause, then he marched back to the stand to watch the rest of the game. Montrose pulled one back within ten minutes of the restart, but that was the last of their contribution to the game. Troup himself scored another for Forfar and the game fizzled out in the lovely summer sunshine with Forfar well on top.

It was also lovely summer sunshine across the English Channel at Mons where the first major engagement of the war was taking place. There was as yet no great emotional pressure on young men who didn't want to enlist, for the war was still young and nobody knew what was to come. Although the *Forfar Dispatch* editorial did deplore the fact that 'the dogs of war have been unleashed', as many column inches were devoted to walks in Clova, millinery fashions, votes for women and whether Surrey would win the County Championship.

Nor was there as yet any great feeling that football should stop for the war. Forfar's next game was to be a local derby against Dundee Hibs at Tannadice Park. (Dundee Hibs was, of course, the original name for Dundee United). A special train would be run from Forfar Station to Dundee next Saturday and the price would be 1s 2d. The *Dispatch* predicted that the team would be the same that beat Montrose i.e. Scott; E. Ferguson and D. Ferguson; Nichol, Chapman and Leighton; Mitchell, Walker, Langlands, Troup and Petrie.

By the time that December came, a more sombre note had been introduced. The phrase 'all over by Christmas' now had a hollow ring to it. Christmas had almost come and the war was still in evidence. Men, including a few from Forfar, had lost their lives. More had come home wounded, in some cases seriously. For them the war was over. The British Expeditionary Force had saved Paris, of that there seemed little doubt, but they had not been able to force themselves into Germany to deliver a major counter-attack. Two lines of opposing trenches, about 100 yards from each other, now ranged from the North Sea to neutral Switzerland. In chess, it would be described as stalemate.

The British propaganda machines did not portray it that way of course. Newspapers were employed to encourage yet more men to join the great adventure. Was Alec tempted at this point? Probably yes, but there was so much to do at home. He enjoyed his work as a plasterer, there was a young lady called Elizabeth Kidd who was interested in him and he in her, and there was also his football. How he was enjoying himself! In any case, he was young enough. He was not yet twenty. There would be time yet.

The game against Montrose in the Forfarshire Cup at Station Park in the rain on 19 December was a poor one but the *Dispatch* records:

> The only outstanding incident of the match was the scoring of a great goal by Troup. It was an effort worthy of McLean: an unexpected drive from long range directed at the part of the goal where it was most likely to take effect. The goalkeeper was handicapped by the gathering darkness, but, tall as he was, it is doubtful if he could have held the ball even under favourable conditions. In addition to the plaudits of the crowd and the congratulations of his comrades, the feat brought Troup the compliment of a sportsmanlike handshake from one of his opponents.

Forfar were playing in two leagues this year – the Northern and the Central. It was small wonder that they managed to complete their fixtures in either league, for the war restrictions on when football could be played were strict. Midweek games were frowned upon, lest they encourage idleness in the work force. In the event, Forfar would eventually be declared winners of the Northern League, although neither they nor anyone else had finished their programme!

But Troup was a joy to watch. 1915's New Year's Day game at Gayfield, Arbroath finished in a 2-2 draw, but 'Troup played cleverly', according to *The Courier*. On 2 January, when Bathgate came to Station Park, Troup scored 'with a splendid shot after grand individual work, and with a little luck he might have had his customary brace'. The *Forfar Herald* adds that 'he revelled in the mud and delighted the spectators with his trickery and surprise pots at goal'. Troup's goal was the only goal of the game, and this became a pattern for the rest of the season. For Forfar to win, it required Troup to play well and, for preference, to score. This happened against King's Park on 30 January, for example, when 'Troup put up his usual grand display'.

In March, Forfar went out of the Forfarshire Cup to Arbroath with 'Troup only of the five forwards impressing', but as the season came to an end, there were signs that the team, in spite of leading the Northern League and being well positioned in the Central, were losing heart. Crowds were dropping and secretary James Black was now openly saying that there might not be a Forfar Athletic next season, as he thought everyone should be 'doing their bit' for God, King and Country, encouraging even his own committee men and players to join up, he himself being over forty and a trifle too old. He also decided that soldiers and sailors could attend Forfar's games when home on leave and get in for half-price.

On 10 April, Troup and 'Jummer' Petrie, the Forfar left wing, impressed in a game at Dens Park in a game against Dundee 'A', but there was precious little else to get excited about. It was a game, however, which would have an effect on Troup's future, for eyebrows were raised in the Dundee directors' box at the play of the young Forfarian. In a 1-1 draw against Aberdeen 'A' on 17 April, Troup only occasionally gave glimpses of his cleverness, and a week later the team lost 0-1 at Tannadice to Dundee Hibs, who featured in their line-up the curiously named Herbert Dainty, who had been Dundee's centre half when they won the cup in their golden year of 1910. The Tannadice game was 24 April, and as war-time regulations forbade professional football after the end of April (lest it interfere with the war effort and the munitions industry), Forfar's last game of the season (and for several seasons afterwards) appears to have been a friendly against a select XI of the local juniors, in which Troup inspired the Athletic to win 4-1.

In a dressing room tinged with sadness after the game, several men stated their intention to join up. Once again Alec felt pressurised, but once again he resisted the moral blackmail. The *Forfar Herald* joined in the pressure by printing a list of Forfarians who were in the colours, and those whose names were not there could be noticed. It was not that he had any conscientious objection to the war (Alec knew full well in any case that the 'conshies' had a tougher time than the ordinary soldier), it was just that he was a home-loving lad and he enjoyed what he did and he loved Forfar. He was now twenty, but he still had no great desire to move. He felt no need to join up. He preferred playing football to killing Germans and running the risk of being killed himself.

Mind you, he was going to miss his 'futba' if Black carried out his threat to put the club in abeyance. There was already a precedent in the town in that the Strathmore Cricket Club were not playing any games in the summer of 1915. But there would be some sort of football for him to play on a Saturday afternoon, wouldn't there? There had been stories for over a year that teams like Dundee and Aberdeen had shown an interest in him. Now would be a nice time for them to come knocking on his door – otherwise he might have to join up, for the only benefit that he could think of joining the colours was that all these battalions and regiments had football teams.

But his decision was made for him one day in early August, when Black announced that there would be no football in Forfar this coming year. It was not unconnected with this decision that four well-dressed, burly men drove in a car from Dundee to Forfar. This was an unusual event in 1915, for cars were rare and petrol in wartime was scarce. They drove to the house in Queen Street (where the car was immediately surrounded by curious urchins), asked for Alec Troup and were told by his mother that he was out on a job. Her visitors were Mr William McIntosh of Dundee Football Club and three of his henchmen.

# 3

# DUNDEE

Alec was working up a ladder repairing a roof in the yard of a joiner and undertaker called Henry Dall at the East Port. On hearing a cry of 'Are you there, Alec Troup?' and seeing the well-dressed Dundonians, Alec immediately wiped his hands and came down the ladder. His first concern, as he would explain later, was that these men might be detectives wishing to interview him for some alleged breaking of the Defence of the Realm Act.

This piece of legislation (called by its acronym DORA) was a particularly draconian and repressive measure. It gave the police the power to arrest someone for 'unwarlike activities', which could amount to as little as a chance remark along the lines of 'The Germans aren't all that bad' or 'I don't want to join up because I don't see why I should'. Alec was terrified in case he, or someone in his family, might have said something along those lines, and that (Forfar being the gossipy place that it was) the unfortunate remark may have reached the ears of an over-zealous local policeman.

The men, however, smiled and asked him, as Forfar Athletic had now apparently closed down for the duration of the war, if he would like to join Dundee. Financial terms, albeit limited ones, were offered. Alec accepted that, in the circumstances of the war, Dundee were restricted in what they could offer, and there being no further negotiations (other than travelling expenses), he agreed to sign there and then. The delighted Dundee director immediately whipped out the necessary forms for Alec to sign. Alec then looked for a surface on which to sign them and found one – a new coffin! It was a macabre start to his Dundee career.

Forfar Athletic were to receive not a penny in a transfer fee. They were now in abeyance and, for some reason or other, did not pursue the matter in 1919 when perhaps legal action might well have compelled Dundee to pay up. Dundee, in fact, did very well out of this deal. They had kept an eye on Troup for some time, and his fine performance in the game on 10 April 1915 at Dens Park against their reserve team in the Northern League might well have been what decided them to go for Troup, particularly as he appeared to be totally free. The legal implications were uncertain in these unusual and unprecedented circumstances.

Thus Alec Troup joined Dundee in the summer of 1915. To play professional football with a First Division club was, of course, the dream of any youngster, and Alec (who had only just turned twenty) jumped at the chance. In 1915, the First Division was what it said it was – the home of the best clubs in Scotland. It wasn't until sixty years later, with the appearance of the 'Premier' League, that the words

'First Division' were demeaned. Dundee was the logical place for any Forfarian to go. It was only fifteen miles to the south of Forfar, and in no real sense, given the disparity in size between the two towns, was there any rivalry between the two places. They were like big brother and little brother as it were, and travel between the two of them since the opening of the railway link in 1870 had been cheap and easy. The railway line stayed open until 1955, when competition from the much more flexible buses brought about its closure.

Forfarians would be warned (and not entirely without cause) of the dangers to one's body and soul in the large metropolis of Dundee, with its dens of iniquity, fleshpots and daughters of Jezabel on the street. Dundonians, on the other hand, would make jokes about Forfar's steeple which was covered with a tent when the rain came on. When a man said that he came from Forfar, the answer often was 'Well, somebody has to, I suppose!' or 'You get tae dae that, of coorse!' The story is told of the Dundonian about to marry a Forfar girl and being warned off because of her versatility in the past on the grounds that 'Half o' Farfar's been oot wi' her'. 'I ken' he said, 'but Farfar's just a wee place!'. In spite of all this, there was a genuine affection between Forfar and Dundee, brought about by many generations of intermarriage. Troup's own parents, of course, had been married in Dundee in 1872.

In footballing terms, the whole of Angus (or Forfarshire, as it was then called) had been set alight by Dundee's magnificent performance in 1910 when they won the Scottish Cup in a twice-replayed final against Clyde. Forfarian Geordie Langlands (nicknamed 'Purkie', for some obscure reason) had played for Dundee, and indeed it had been his late goal that had earned Dundee a draw in the first game. Geordie, of course, was now back in Forfar and played with Troup in his two seasons at Station Park.

But Troup's move to Dundee (which in normal circumstances would have been a dream scenario) was tinged with unreality, for these were not normal times. The war had been on for a year, Forfar Athletic had decided to close down for the duration, and if Alec wanted to play any professional football at all, he would have to move. Of course, full-time football was not allowed by regulations, and wages were strictly limited, even to part-timers. Alec was legally still a plasterer, and football was merely a supplement to his earnings.

In any case, there was a growing feeling that football as a whole would do better to close down for the duration of the war. It was now clear by the summer of 1915 that the war was to be a long one, and the casualty lists in the two Dundee papers – *The Courier* and *The Advertiser* – and Forfar's *Dispatch* and *Herald* (although the lists of dead and wounded were by no means as bad as they would become in 1917 and 1918) were hammering home this message. Last year's moonshine about 'over by Christmas' was now replaced by grim realism, which British propaganda for all its 'successes' and 'pushes' was unable to mask.

Restrictions were everywhere, although Forfar was situated in one of the most fertile farming areas of Great Britain and would not be too badly affected by any threat of food shortages. After the war, Dr Lowson, the man in charge of local food supplies, would boast that, on several occasions, Forfar had been able to send food to the Army and Navy over and above the normal 'quota'. This had been done by encouraging farmers and the local population in general to cultivate ever single square yard of land to produce potatoes and carrots. Forfar was a veritable 'land of Goshen', said Dr Lowson, who clearly enjoyed hyperbole as well as possessing a thorough knowledge of his Bible. Goshen was the land of plenty in the books of Genesis and Exodus.

Letters, however, appeared frequently in newspapers stating that it was 'unpatriotic' to play football, and why were twenty-two fit young men not wearing khaki? Alec may well have been the subject of a few unkind comments about 'plastering' during the week, and 'plastering' as well on a Saturday by playing football, when so many other young men were facing the foe.

Yet there was a counter argument. It was surely necessary to provide the civilian population with some kind of relief from the horrors of war. Men home on leave deserved to see and play in some kind of sport. Music halls, theatres and cinemas were still open, and Charlie Chaplin was beginning to became a far greater hero than Kitchener, whose pointing finger still told everyone that their country needed them. After all, one of the greatest musical hits of the war was 'Keep The Home Fires Burning'. Such fires were more likely to be kept alight if the population was being entertained.

These arguments may well have been discussed at length in the Troup household. It is hard to believe that Alec's mother, who had acted so valiantly to defend him against Sunny Jim, would have been in any way willing to see him go off to fight in a war. He was her youngest and dearest. Alec had decided that he would sign for Dundee (it had been by no means a secret, long before their meeting in the joiner's yard, that they were toying with the idea of asking him) and continue his job as a plasterer ... at least for the time being. His full-back colleague at Forfar Athletic, Ernie Ferguson, had already done the same thing. He would also play part-time for Dundee, and continue his job in the factory. Both Forfarians played in Dundee's trial match on Wednesday 18 August, and clearly impressed them well enough for Dundee to give them a game on Saturday.

In spite of the very unusual circumstances of his signing, it was a proud moment for Mr and Mrs Ben Troup on 21 August 1915 when Alec made his first-team debut for Dundee against Ayr United at Dens Park. His father was still far from happy at the thought of his son playing professional football, but he probably reconciled himself to the idea by reckoning that he couldn't stop him anyway, and that he was, temporarily at least, away from German artillery. He had seen a few games at Station Park the previous season, and indeed enjoyed the reflected glory of being the father of such a great local hero. 'He learned it all from me,' he would joke. Seriously, he was beginning to develop an affection for the game that he had never before possessed, even when his elder son Dave played for Forfar.

Yet, the crowd at Dens Park at Alec's debut was little over 5,000 – a poor crowd for the First Division in comparison with pre-war days, and the atmosphere was lacking. Minds were elsewhere. Dundee, however, won 2-0, and Troup scored a brilliant goal which the *Courier* describes thus:

> There was an outstandingly brilliant goal, scored by Troup, the young lad got from Forfar. Nobody expected it, least of all Kerr the Ayr custodian. Troup was tackled as he pounced on the ball, but tipped the leather

behind him, and turning round, drove the ball hard and true into the visitors' goal.

The *Forfar Herald*, which, of course, had no Forfar game to report on, commented that:

> The loon's goal was a beauty. Gordon Kerr never imagined that a stripling of a youth could drive with such force from twenty yards out. He gave a glance towards Troup as much as to say "What are you doing shooting from that distance?" When Troup received a drooping pass, he simply swung round and at the correct moment booted the ball goalwards.

Troup also assisted in the other goal, which centre forward Davie Brown scored. It was a good start for 'Eckie', whom the Dundee crowd had already taken to their hearts. The *Courier* states concisely: 'Troup was the star, of course'. Enigmatically, however, the scribe adds that he should remember that 'Steven is not a winger'– and he wasn't, of course. George Steven was a fine inside man, played out of position by necessity. Troup was playing at inside left in those early days. It would take a while before this particular penny would drop with the Dundee management. The team on Eckie's debut was Balfour; Ferguson and Aitken; McIntosh, McDonald and Stirling; Fisher, McCulloch, Brown, Troup and Steven.

Troup played at inside left in every game that autumn of 1915 until early December. The fortunes of the team were indifferent. Reports on Troup's form varied. A defeat at Cappielow on 28 August had the *Courier* writer in despair about the general form of the team, but nevertheless 'the Dundee management are to be congratulated on their capture of Troup and Ferguson' – a phrase that must have gone down particularly well among its Forfar readership. On 4 September, however, following a bad home defeat at the hands of Motherwell, Troup was 'too light to be any use against the Motherwell halves, who were heavy but by no means slow'. The following week, after a win at Airdrie, Troup scored a 'capital goal' but was damned with faint praise. 'Troup was all right, so long as he restricted his individualistic tendencies.'

On 18 September came Dundee's first really big game of the season: the visit of Celtic to Dens Park. Even in wartime circumstances this was a great occasion, for Celtic were the champions for the previous two years and sparkled with great players such as Young, Gallacher and McMenemy, who remembered Eckie from that great day at Station Park before the war. Celtic's manager Maley took no chances and assigned the tough-tackling McMaster and Johnstone, rather than Sunny Jim Young, to deal with Troup. Celtic's two cluggers had learned a lesson from that game a year past February. Dundee lost 0-2 and sadly, Troup's 'cleverness availed nothing'. Sunny Jim shook Alec's hand at the end, then added with a smile 'Ah hope your mither's no here the day, Alec', whilst glancing anxiously round the crowd.

It was a different story the following week when another Glasgow team – Queen's Park – appeared. Troup was absolutely magnificent that day. He scored twice himself and played a part in most of Davie Brown's five, as Dundee beat the amateurs (as Queen's Park were and still, to their credit, remain) 7-1. He showed a 'great deal of cleverness', and had the Dens Park fans in raptures. As he walked off the park that day, he was congratulated by a Queen's Park player, whom Troup remembered for having had a few good runs down the left wing in an otherwise lifeless Queen's Park forward line. 'Well played, Mr Troup. My name's Morton – Alan Morton'. They would meet again.

Troup was still playing at inside left all this time. A weakness of his game, if there was one, was that his small frame tended to be knocked out of the way in the melée in the centre of the park. This happened against Motherwell, Hearts and Kilmarnock. It is noticeable that reports of his play began to say less and less in the month of November. Against Hearts on 6 November, he was 'as usual clever and a valuable aid to Brown' but during the next few weeks, he was barely mentioned, other than in the general criticism of the team.

Alec himself began to feel (as did some of his Forfar admirers who had watched his career from the early days) that he might be better in the wide open spaces of the left wing, where he would have more room to beat his man and then round him before sending over a cross, particularly the slow hanging cross at which he excelled.

Circumstances brought this about in any case. He was injured in a game against Partick Thistle at Firhill on 4 December 1915 (where his 'shooting was wretched') before a hefty charge did a great deal of damage to his already weak collarbone. This was something that he had problems with before, and as a result of this, he had to play every game from then on with his collarbone heavily strapped up. However, the more immediate effect, after his return from injury, was a change of position.

He was once again available for selection by the middle of January 1916. Manager William Wallace decided that Troup should be experimented with on the left wing at the expense of Sid Lamb, while George Steven, who had played so well at inside left in Troup's absence, should be persevered with in that position.

Wallace backed his judgement on this issue, even if the opponents on 15 January 1916 were to be Rangers. In all truth, Rangers were much ravaged by the war and were far from a vintage Ibrox side. This became apparent at Dens Park that day, when Troup ran them ragged with a series of dribbles, followed by a change of pace to get to the dead-ball line, and then a brilliant dropping cross to the eager head of Brown or Steven. Brown scored twice that day, and Rangers were lucky to get off with a 2-0 defeat.

Alec would be less successful against Celtic. He was destined to have his moments against them as well, but on 28 February at Parkhead he found himself up against the great Alec McNair. McNair – who, in later years, would become the manager of Dundee – was a gentlemanly player, unlike the more brutal Young and McMaster. Playing as elegantly as always, McNair never gave Troup a kick of the ball, and all Troup could do was admire the brilliance of the Patsy Gallacher-inspired Celtic team of that period, as they routed Dundee 3-0.

Attendances towards the end of the 1915/16 season continued to be poor at Dens Park, averaging out at about 5,000, and even Rangers and Celtic were struggling to top 10,000. This was simply because those who would normally have been at such games were wearing khaki in a trench in France. There was no Scottish Cup during the war, and this meant the only games played were League games, and perhaps friendlies. Strange things happened as well. As football was not normally allowed in midweek (lest it interfere with attendance at the all-important munitions factories), teams sometimes were compelled to play twice on the Saturday. Famously, Celtic did this on 15 April, beating Raith Rovers 6-0 in the afternoon, then going to Motherwell to win 3-1 in the evening!

Dundee didn't do that, but on several occasions kick-off had to be delayed as the opposition's train was late. Occasionally, a tannoy appeal was made for anyone who had 'ever refereed in junior or school football' to appear at the pavilion, for there might be a job for him! Even the reporting of games in newspapers shows the strain put upon services by the war. On 1 April 1916, for example, Dundee visited Raith Rovers for a local derby. They went on to win 2-0, and the anonymous writer in the *Fife Free Press*, presumably covering for the regular who was in the Armed Forces, moaned about the play of Raith Rovers (not without cause, for they were to end up bottom in the League). But he then goes on to say: 'The Dundee forward line, indeed, was not much better, Brown, Thomson and Troupe (sic) both failing badly in front of goal'.

The mis-spelling of Alec's name is understandable. Perhaps the writer was thinking of a 'troupe of artistes', for example; in fact other writers, under the influence of military terminology would call him 'Alec Troop'. But the writer should surely have paid a little more attention at grammar lessons when he was at school. He should have known that the English word 'both' can only be used with two commodities, not three!

Dundee finished eighth in the twenty-team League, but football seemed to matter little in these times. 1916 was a very sobering stage in the war effort, and people were becoming less and less convinced by the propaganda that they read in newspapers about 'pushes' and 'advances'. The Western Front seemed to be holding, but the Russians (Britain's unlikely allies) were doing less well in the east, and the Allies had lost many men the previous year at the Dardanelles. The same papers that had been singing the praises of the British High Command now contained ever-growing lists of casualties. Inevitably, in a small town like Forfar, some of the casualties were men known personally to Troup, including one or two who had been to school with him or played football for North End at the Market Muir in happier days.

On two occasions in the spring of 1916, the war came uncomfortably close to Forfar. On the evening of Sunday 2 April, church bells (including Forfar's famous 'Lang Strang') pealed. Normally, the bells were silenced under DORA, except to summon the special constables. Forfarians wondered what was happening, and then a few minutes later came the droning but ever-increasing sound of Zeppelins. Already there had been a few raids on London, and that very night there was a raid on Leith docks in Edinburgh. Mothers panicked and hid children in cupboards, while they themselves prayed and extinguished all lights. Why the Zeppelins visited Angus, no one ever found out. It was probably a reconnaissance mission, but it did terrify the population, many of whom had never even seen an aeroplane before, let alone a Zeppelin. A similar event occurred exactly a month later – and again no explanation was forthcoming.

By this time, however, a platform had been built on top of the Peel monument in Forfar cemetery – a construction which allowed soldiers an unrestricted view of most of Angus. However, the night of 2 May was dull and misty, and neither did Forfarians see Zeppelins, nor did the Germans see Forfar, apparently. There was, however, that drone, relentless and monotonous, which the young children of 1916 would remember all their lives.

On the broader front, the spring of 1916 saw two dreadful events. In April the Irish in Dublin rebelled and were brutally repressed. Then at the end of May came the naval disaster of the Battle of Jutland. At the time, of course, it was another 'great victory'. More soberly, it is described in history books as an 'indecisive battle'. So it was, in that neither the British nor the Germans cleared the other from the North Sea or any place else. In fact, it was a bad defeat for both, and the loss of life was horrendous.

Even worse was to come on land in mid-summer. General Douglas Haig saw the river Somme as the ideal place for an offensive on 1 July. Little had been done to check the positions and strength of the German artillery. Whistles were blown at 6 a.m. in the morning, men went over the top, and those who refused were often shot there and then by their own officers. Ninety minutes later (the length of a football match), the equivalent of the attendances at six Dundee home games lay dead and dying in an orgy of carnage, something which is difficult to parallel in the history of military warfare, and remains to this day the saddest single event in the history of the British army.

The discrepancy between banner headlines in newspapers and reality could not have been more acute. The *Courier* on 4 July 1916 talks about 'Brilliant Allied Success', and the next day runs the headline 'Hitting Huns All Round'. Yet already these two editions contain stories of families from Cowdenbeath, Brechin and Montrose with losses of young men. A family from Dundee itself 'patriotically' lost two sons on the same day. One man's wife gave birth, then was told that her husband was 'missing', a euphemism for being blown apart. A young boy ran home in triumph from a Kirkcaldy primary school – having been told that he had won the Dux medal – only to find his mother in tears with a crumpled telegram in her hands.

Forfar suffered awfully. The story ran around the town of the soldier whose wife had not been able to go the station a couple of weeks earlier to see him off. She was assisting (as an amateur midwife) in the birth of her neighbour's child. But just as the soldier was walking down the street in Newmonthill, resplendent in his kilt in the warm June sunshine, kitbag over his shoulder, he heard a knock on the window. He turned back and there was his wife holding up a little baby girl, born seconds previously. He smiled, waved back, glad that Belle's confinement had gone well and thought that the baby would have grown by the time he was back – but he never came back.

Yet such was the strength of British propaganda that there was still no great anti-war feeling. The churches still backed it, even allowing people to work on the Sabbath if it was for the war effort. A few voices in the infant Labour party raised their voices to protest, but they were quickly marginalised. Feelings ran strong, but not against the warmongers like Lloyd George, Churchill or Haig – they were, after all, representing 'King and Country'. Even less was it against the real perpetrators of evil, the war profiteers who were doing very nicely from the sale of shells and bullets. The demons (in the eyes of the hysterical populace) were the German, the Irish, the pacifists, the conscientious objectors and the war dodgers.

Troup's conscience was now beginning to get the better of him, and he was coming under real pressure. Now twenty-one, he could no longer plead his age as an excuse for not enlisting. He was indeed a war dodger. He was aware of people's stares, and he certainly found it hard to look the war widows in the eye and at those who had returned, in some cases permanently disfigured. Those who admired his prowess on the football field would often ask quite openly why he was not in uniform. He certainly would not escape for ever. Conscription had now been legalised for several months, and it was only a matter of time before he would be told, as opposed to being asked or encouraged, to join the colours.

Alec could, of course, say that he was still plying his trade as a plasterer, and that there would always be a need for house repairs at home. On the other hand, a friend of his was a baker and used the same excuse until he was 'persuaded' that the Royal Flying Corps in far away Palestine and Mesopotamia would need cooks.

For the moment, however, this took a back seat while personal matters took over. July 1916 saw a devastating blow fall on the Troup family. Benjamin, who had been in indifferent health for some time, died at the age of sixty-four. He was suffering from prostate cancer and cystitis. He had known for some time that there was a problem – his 'waterworks' had given him a lot of trouble – but he did not necessarily suspect that it was to be fatal. A genuine and sincere man, Ben had been worn down by the stress of the war. Two of his sons were in the forces, and he was appalled at the senseless slaughter of it all. He died in his family home in the early hours of 21 July, much loved and respected by his family, friends and neighbours.

It had such an effect on Alec that he postponed any decision about 'joining up'. He felt that his mother needed him – for the time being at least. Very soon, he was well aware that he would have no choice, for conscription would eventually catch up with him, but he wanted to stay with his mother for a while. She herself had been failing, and even though she was still in her early sixties there were clear signs that the mind was beginning to go. More and more she pined for 'puir little Geordie', the baby who had died in infancy, and she would not be consoled about the loss of the strong man in her family, her beloved Ben.

When the 1916/17 football season started again in August, life became even more chaotic for Alec and for Dundee FC. They were victims of their own geography, for it was difficult to get their men together to travel to the west. Not only that, but they could never rely on their own men, even for home games. Wartime transport had started off being bad, and was now palpably deteriorating, with branch-lines such as that from Dundee to Forfar clearly a very low priority. If an engine broke down, for example, it stayed broken down until other more urgent matters, like the transport of soldiers or supplies, were attended to.

Yet the games that Troup did manage to turn out in were good ones as far as he was concerned. He had a great game against Hibs at Easter Road on 16 September, and scored a fine goal, and the weekend after that in a draw against Airdrie at Dens Park, he and the other winger Jim Herron were 'the best of the forwards'. Then after that he was 'unable to travel' to Glasgow for a game against Queen's Park, and was similarly missing for a home game against Falkirk.

But the game that possibly persuaded Troup that football in wartime was a dead loss and that 'joining up' was perhaps a more viable option, was the game played at

Greenock Morton on 14 October 1916. He managed to get the train from Forfar Station at 7.54 a.m. to take him to Dundee, and then at 8.45 a.m. the Dundee team left Tay Bridge Station to go to Glasgow, and then on to Port Glasgow where they changed to a 'car' (a tramcar) to take them to Cappielow. There had been numerous delays on the trains, which were heavily thronged with naval and military personnel going on leave or returning from it, and the rain lashed down incessantly. When the team reached Greenock at 2 p.m. for a 3 p.m. kick-off, the pitch was more or less under water. 'It always does rain in Greenock', they say, and it certainly did that day.

The pitch was clearly unplayable, but such was the situation of wartime (where a midweek replay of the game was totally impossible) that they decided to go ahead anyway. Ludicrously, it was also believed that the postponement of a game might give the enemy vital information about weather conditions! German spies with concealed radios and telephones were said to be everywhere. In a travesty of a game, in which only Troup's wing in the first half was anything like playable, Morton won 1-0.

The players now had to return to Dundee. The tramcar line to Port Glasgow station was under water and the service had been suspended. But if the team did not make the 5.45 p.m. train, then there was no chance of getting back to Dundee that day. So, they had to run through puddles. They did so, and at one point Alec Troup misjudged the depth of what seemed to be a small puddle and plunged right in! They reached Port Glasgow station, but the train was an hour late. It arrived, but was further delayed in Glasgow, Stirling and Perth, so that the team eventually got home to Dundee well after midnight, and Alec had to stay the night in Napper Thomson's house, soaked, miserable and feeling that life in the trenches could hardly be much worse than that.

Troup now realised that even though conscription had been introduced, it had not yet reached him. Indeed, he had some leeway. He was a plasterer by trade, and such expertise would be of great benefit to regiments like the Royal Engineers. He put this point to the recruiting officer on the Monday evening, and the point was taken. Troup filled in a few forms, was told that he would hear soon about medical examinations and the like, and went back home to nurse the chill that he had picked up from his Greenock experience.

Dundee's form, like their team line-up, continued to be sporadic and unpredictable. On 21 October, they recorded their first home win against Hamilton Accies, with Troup being 'rather too tricky on the wing, although his crosses were good'. On 4 November, 'something like old-time enthusiasm' brought 14,000 to Dens to see Celtic in a game where Troup proved once again that he was no inside left. George Steven got injured and he and Troup changed places. 'Troup was fair on the wing, but at inside left too light to be dangerous', said the *Courier*. Yet the lesson was not learned. On 25 November, he was exchanged with McCulloch to become an inside right and was guilty of some 'rank bad shooting' as the team went down 0-3 to Partick Thistle.

Troup was in and out of the team, at times being unavailable for personal reasons, and missed Dundee's spectacular thumping of Raith Rovers on 9 December when Davie Brown scored all 6 of Dundee's goals. But by that time, two other things were happening. The Liberal government of Asquith had been replaced by a coalition one led by David Lloyd George – hailed by the *Courier* as 'Britain's man of action' – and Troup's call-up papers for the Royal Engineers had come through.

His last game before leaving for basic training at Largs on the Ayrshire coast was against Hearts at Tynecastle on 16 December, where he was 'quiet' in a 1-0 defeat of which the *Advertiser* says that 'it was a good game in the first half, but the pace dropped significantly in the second, a consequence, one presumes, of the inability of players to do meaningful training'.

This was not quite Troup's last game for Dundee before the end of the war, however. On 3 February 1917, Dundee were at Ayr, and Troup, given the proximity of Largs and Ayr, would be available. His commanding officer, presumably himself a football fan and delighted that one of his men was a professional footballer, gave him permission, and so Alec took the field at Somerset Park where he was 'steady and reliable' in a 'thin affair' which Dundee won 2-1.

This game temporarily ended Troup's first spell with Dundee. Dundee struggled along and finished fifth bottom of a League which meant less and less. Raith Rovers, for example, came to Ayr one day without a goalkeeper. Ayr, ever willing to oblige, gave them one of theirs! And Alec Troup was able to get a few games for Ayr United as a 'guest' before the end of the season. On 3 March, Ayr approached Dundee for permission to play Troup in their game against Morton. Dundee had no objection, and thus the following team took the field at Somerset Park to lose 0-3 to Morton in a dire game: Nisbet, Bell and Hay; Waddell, W. Cringan and McLaughlan; R. Cringan, Crosbie, McKenzie, Shankly and Troup. It was a team of a few interesting players – the centre half Willie Cringan would go on to play for Celtic and Scotland after the war, and the inside left was one Alex Shankly, elder brother of the famous Bob and Bill. Bob, of course, managed Dundee when they won the Scottish League in 1962, and Bill Shankly became the legendary manager of Liverpool.

Troup was required for unspecified military duties on 10 March, but played again for Ayr the following week when he came in as inside left for the unavailable Alex Shankly. Ayr beat St Mirren 2-1 that day. He missed out on the next game, but had two matches at outside left on 31 March (a 4-3 defeat by Third Lanark) and on 7 April (a 1-1 draw against Queen's Park). He 'could not get away to play' in the next match, and his reason for missing the following game was that he was 'being inoculated'. However, on the last game of the month, he made his final appearance for Ayr United in a friendly against Kilmarnock, which Ayr lost 0-2.

Thus ended Alec's very short and not very successful career with Ayr United, but in any case, football was now bordering on the absurd. It was sad, but no real loss when Dundee, Raith Rovers and Aberdeen (for geographical and logistic reasons), were asked to leave the League at the end of the season. Dundee then played the 1917/18 season in an Eastern Division (which they won), but even that ended the following season, and Dundee went into abeyance, although Troup was still registered as a player with them.

# 4

# TROUP IN THE TROOPS

Troup's service in the First World War was with the Royal Engineers. The Sappers, as they are sometimes called, are notoriously difficult for any historian to pin down because their job is to help all three services, and they are likely to be anywhere. Indeed, the motto given to them by King William IV in the 1820s was 'Ubique' – the Latin word for 'everywhere', signifying that they have taken part in every battle fought by the British Army in all parts of the world.

As far as the First World War is concerned, the website of the Royal Engineers has this to say about their role: 'With huge armies in the field, the Royal Engineers expanded and raised many specialist units to undertake work normally done by civilians. Engineer units built and maintained camps, stores and depots, provided water and sanitation, supplied timber and stone, built and operated docks and railways and manufactured many items required by the Army. Responsibilities included gas and chemical warfare, air defence searchlights, tunnelling, mining, meteorology, postal services and wireless communications.'

Some time before Christmas in 1916, Troup reported to the Royal Engineers base at Largs on the Ayrshire coast for basic training. His trade as a plasterer would stand him in good stead for a contribution to the war effort, but the first few weeks were spent doing things like marching, running up and down hills (something that the athletic Troup would have had less difficulty with than most) and gymnastics. He also had to take his turn at making and serving the meals, and there would have been countless inoculations against all sorts of diseases.

So what did Troup actually do during the war? We cannot say with any great certainty. He was certainly still in Scotland until the end of the 1916/17 season, for he played a few games for Ayr United. There is not a single trace of him having played any football in Scotland the following season, but there exists a photograph of him in a team group of the Royal Engineers. It also says 'France' on the ball, so it is reasonable to assume that that is where he was.

Records are hard to trace and it seems that Troup's service record in the Royal Engineers was destroyed by a Second World War Luftwaffe bomb at the Record Office at Kew, near London. Unaccountably, the otherwise excellent book *Forfar in the Great War* by David Mackie does not contain Alec's name in the list of those who served. This must be a mistake, for serve he certainly did – and indeed Mackie, in his role as 'The Drummer' in the *Forfar Dispatch*, mentions Troup's military service more than once.

To serve in France in 1917 was no picnic, and 1918 was the year in which the

*Alec during the First World War, playing for '13th Reinforcement Company, Royal Engineers, France', according to the inscription on the ball. Alec is second from left, in the middle row.*

Germans almost won the war. The Ludendorff offensive of spring 1918 represented Germany's last desperate effort for victory, and for a month or two, the British were driven back until, with American support, the tide was turned. An interesting comment was made by one veteran in the 'march back', as the temporary retreat in spring and early summer 1918 was called. At one point, they saw the sea. They were delighted, for the sight of the sea meant that they might be going home sooner rather than later. The fact that they were losing seemed to be of minor significance. One recalls the famous scene in Xenophon's *Anabasis* of the early fourth century BC, when 10,000 Greek mercenaries saw the sea. The Greek word for the sea, 'thalassa', was heard as the soldiers burst into tears of uncontrollable joy. The Greeks, like the British, did not like to be far away from the sea.

No doubt Alec (and millions like him) would have felt the same. He was not by nature a soldier. He was proud of his service, reasonably patriotic and conscious of his duty to his nation. But he would have far preferred the football field to the battle field. Perhaps he did get to play quite a lot of football, for the only picture of him known to exist in the First World War shows him in the football jersey of the Royal Engineers. Germany would eventually surrender on 11 November 1918, but until that time, casualties continued to be heavy. In fact, the worst time for British casualties (if we discount the horrendously ill-thought-out Battle of the Somme and some equally desperate efforts in 1917) was the last few months of the war. Had the Americans not arrived, brought into the war by Germany's insensitive sinking of the *Lusitania* in 1915 and their declaration of unrestricted submarine warfare in 1917, the stalemate and slaughter would have continued for many more years.

But the end did come, on 11 November 1918. Rumours had abounded in the newspapers and conversation for a few days. Everyone's mood had changed. The all-embracing depression had given way to animation and even a little desperate optimism. It was an archetypal Scottish November Monday morning. Foggy, raw, not desperately cold, drizzly and dark. Forfar East School was in session. The teacher was not liked. About thirty-five and not unattractive but forbiddingly dressed in black with a long, plaited skirt, she seldom smiled, except after she had given some poor little character the belt for his inability to spell words like 'meadow'.

They were doing the seven times table, chanting 'seven sevens are forty nine', when the door opened, and a man with a moustache came in. This was the headmaster. The class rose up to salute him, chanting 'Good Morning, Headmaster' as the custom was. He smiled and whispered something to Miss Milne, who in turn smiled back. 'Really?' she said. During the animated conversation, 'armistice at 11 o'clock' was eagerly overheard at the front by the ragamuffins who had been put there the previous week for bad behaviour. Suddenly, Miss Milne turned to the class and told them to go out into the playground.

Amazed and relieved at getting a break from their drudgery, but not yet totally aware of the significance of it all, everyone trooped out. There they saw a boy wearing the Boy Scout's uniform with a bicycle. In his hand he had a piece of paper. Teachers and pupils clamoured to see it, and one word was uppermost in the buzz. It was 'armistice'. 'There's an armistice! They've signed the armistice! The Huns have surrendered'. There was cheering and joy, tears and hugs. An older boy came out of the school with a bell and was told to run up and down the street as far as the Volunteer Arms, ringing it. 'The war's ower!' cried everyone. 'Ma ded'll be back the morn's nicht,' cried one optimist. Another boy cried, for his father would never return.

The end of the war did not necessarily bring the end to all the suffering. Far from it, for all sorts of small wars continued as a by-product of the main show, notably in Russia, where the British continued to give support to the White Russians or counter-revolutionaries; in the Middle East theatre of war, where Britain's inability to bring about peace and reconciliation would be a constant source of trouble for the rest of the century and longer; and in Ireland, where the ferocity would not abate for some considerable time.

For Alec, though, the war was indeed over, and throughout the early months of 1919, soldiers began to trickle home to their families – in Alec's case to his widowed mother and sister and the young lady called Elizabeth Kidd, to whom he had written many letters. The scene of his return, sometime in spring 1919, is perhaps easy to imagine, for it would have been replicated many times. There was a long, slow train journey to Calais, troop ship to Dover, train to London and the hunt at King's Cross station for the train to Forfar. Perhaps he experienced the irrational fear that the train might yet crash and he wouldn't get home after all. There was the slow trek home past Perth, Coupar Angus, Alyth Junction, Glamis then the train passing Station Park on its way into Forfar Station, his dear mother and sister waiting for him, the tears, the embraces, the handshakes from friends, the offers to carry the kitbag – and the sobering thought among all the euphoria that there would be many for whom there was no homecoming. Many mothers and wives would not be at any railway station waiting for someone to return.

The details of Alec's war service are sparse. Records have been destroyed in another war. The very nature of the Royal Engineers means that it is difficult to pin down where any particular member was and all we can say is that Alec was one of the lucky ones to survive. His footballing skills were in no way impaired however, and for that, Dundee, Everton and Scotland could count themselves very lucky indeed.

Like all men who fought in that horrendous conflict, Troup could hardly have been unaffected by what he had seen. However, he apparently seldom talked about it in later life – he was far more interested in his football. He would never forget – and he certainly made a point of being in church every Armistice Day – but it was an episode that he preferred to forget, something that partly at least explains the lack of material that we can find about his role in the 'war to end all wars'.

# 5

# APRÈS LA FIN DE LA GUERRE

When This Lousy War Is Over
No More Soldiering For Me
When I Get My Civvy Clothes On
Oh, How Happy I Will Be!

The war, with all its unimaginable horrors and unspeakable sufferings, technically ended on 11 November 1918. It was an 'Armistice' or 'cessation of fighting' until such time as peace treaties could be 'negotiated'. There was little negotiation, however. The Allies were unforgiving, and dictated humiliating terms, including payment of reparations to their proud, but defeated foes. Such terms came into force at the end of June 1919. The Allies were to some extent planting the seeds for another war twenty years later.

The rejoicing was intense but muted in so many cases by the thought of young lads lying in Flanders fields or the other theatres of war. Victory, if it could be called that, had been achieved at a cost which even now, almost one hundred years later, shocks and astonishes the historian. Lloyd George himself, the hero of the hour, described the year of 1918, in a memorable turn of phrase, as a 'bloodstained stagger to victory'.

But for those who survived, the mood was varied. Throughout 1919, soldiers returned. In some cases, their family circumstances had changed. The devoted wife had on occasion, been somewhat less than that. Babies had grown into cheeky, intolerable brats, lacking paternal guidance in their formative years. Older relatives had died, sometimes through natural causes, occasionally through circumstances brought about by the stress of living through a horrendous war, and frequently from the Spanish flu virus which devastated Europe in late 1918 and early 1919.

The statistics of Forfar are terrifying. A total of 1,930 took part in the conflict and of these, 439 were either killed in action or died in service. This frightening proportion takes no account of the wounded, both seriously and less so, and the gassed who would suffer ill-health for the rest of their shortened lives. Nor can any number be put upon those who suffered personality changes and psychological trauma.

Sometimes, however, the return may have been as ideal as that portrayed in the popular Harry Lauder song of the time:

When the fighting is over, when the battle is won
And the flags are waving free

And all the laddies to their hames will be returning
The laddies who fought for you and me.
And we'll all gather round the old fireside
Ilka mither will boast o' her son
And all the lassies will be kissin' all the laddies
The laddies who fought and won!

One suspects, however, that most homecomings were totally different, for even young men who perhaps had survived the shells and the artillery could hardly have hoped to have totally avoided the mental trauma associated with exposure to constant fear of death and the sight of so many friends and comrades dying or being horrendously wounded. In the case of Sir Harry Lauder himself, for example, there would be no return for his son, Captain John Lauder.

Perhaps more accurate were two beautiful Angus poems written in the aftermath of the war. One was by Violet Jacobs, imagining herself in the place of a bereaved mother. It is called 'Ay, but ye live'.

I canna' see ye, lad, I canna' see ye
For a' yon glory that's aboot yer heid,
Yon licht that haps ye an' the Hosts that's wi' ye.
Ay, but ye live, and it's mysel' that's deid.

They went frae mill an' mart; frae wind-blawn places,
An' grey toon-closes; i' the empty street
Nae mair the bairnies ken their steps, their faces,
Nor stand to listen to the trampin' feet.

Beside the broom and soughin' through the rashes
Yer voice comes back to me at ilka turn,
Across the brae an' whaur the water washes
The arn-tree, wi' its feet amangst the burn.

Whiles, ye come ben the hoose when day is fleein'
And a' the road oot-by is still at nicht,
But weary een like mine is no for seein'
An gin they saw, they wad be blind wi' licht.

Deith canna kill. The mools o' France be o'er ye,
An' yet ye live, O sodger o' the Lord!
For Him that focht wi' sin an' deith afore ye,
He gie'd the life: twas Him that gie's the sword.

Tho, gin ye see my face, or gin ye hear me
I daurna' ask, I dinna seek to ken

E'en tho' I dee o' sic a glory near me,
By nicht or day, come ben, my bairn, come ben!

An even more poignant local poem is 'The Forfar Bus' by J.B. Salmond, a Dundonian ex-serviceman who worked in Forfar. 'The Pillars' was where the bus stance used to be in Dundee.

On the Forfar bus in a morn of spring
A nipping wind and the frost's sharp sting;
And I can't tell why, but you want to sing
If your heart's like the heart o' me.
The folks in the bus, they stretch their legs,
And talk of the fall in the price of eggs,
Of milk by the pint and butter in kegs
With 'Drop in some day to your tea.'

And my mind goes back to the days that were
Days of turmoil and days of stir,
And a bus from Albert to Pozieres
And fellows that rode wi' me.
We cursed the night, and we cursed the wet;
We envied the luck of the men we met
Coming out of the trenches at Courcelette
A deuce of a place to be.

The Forfar bus brought me back once more
As the clock at the Pillars was striking four;
Though the wind may blow and the rain may pour,
There's a chair and a fire for me.
But the lads that jumped off at the duckboard track
(Cold was the night and heavy the pack)
They didn't join on when the bus went back
And they'll never come in for their tea.

Such had been the sense of loss in Forfar that the Town Council set about constructing one of the more striking of the many war memorials that were erected throughout the country at that time. They situated it on nearby Balmashanner Hill and commissioned one of the best local architects of the day, Thomas Souter, to design a tower that would be not unlike Thucydides' 'ktema es aei' – something that would last for ever. The tower was built between 1920 and 1921 and formally opened on Armistice Day 1921, when the whole town appeared to pay tribute to the dead. Those who travel nowadays on the A92 from Dundee to Aberdeen no longer pass through Forfar, but they cannot fail to be impressed by the magnificent structure with its commanding view of the valley of Strathmore.

But for the survivors, life did return. There was often an additional problem to be faced in the horrible illness which became known as 'Spanish flu'. Alec Troup apparently avoided a serious bout of the illness – on this occasion – but it struck the civilian population hard. Plague is, of course, one of the Four Horseman of the Apocalypse in the Book of Revelation in the Bible. At the time, some religious people were not slow to use this illness to their own advantage, averring that God was angry with humans, not for the war (which many considered necessary to defeat the Kaiser, who was considered to be the German Antichrist), but for the laxity in human morals, particularly the sexual indulgences of the soldiers in Paris and London.

More perceptive analysts would talk about the Great Plague of Athens in 430 B.C. and the Black Death which recurred many times through the Middle Ages. The one thing that epidemics and pandemics all had in common (and still do in the Third World in the early twenty-first century) was that they were the by-product of a war, with all the strains that it necessarily imposes on hygiene and food supplies.

When Alec stepped off the train at Forfar station in early 1919, his mother and sister were there to meet him, rightly proud of their 'led' who had done so well in foreign fields. But Alec might well have been struck by how quiet the town was. There were reasons for this – many men who had been there in 1914 were no longer there, their families in town felt it necessary to mourn for them and in 1919 this meant staying in the house – and also a high percentage of the population were ill.

Sometimes children were the only people well enough to run the household, for this illness knew no half measures. The virus prostrated the victims, and in many cases killed them, particularly the very young, the very old or those whose resistance had been weakened by the psychological trauma of what had happened to themselves or their family in what was now called the Great War. People died in such great numbers and such was the fear that corpses could pollute the atmosphere that, most unusually for the times, permission was granted to hold funerals on Sundays.

The disease peaked in February 1919, then eased off with the appearance of the warmer weather. Now ex-soldiers, heroes all, could be seen on the streets, smiling and earning plaudits from the women, old and young. Yet there was not a single ex-serviceman, for all his swagger, who did not bear some sort of scar, be it physical or emotional, underneath the surface.

Troup's return to his tearful mother in Forfar in early 1919 meant that he could resume his football career with Dundee, with whom he was still a player. The problem was that Dundee had been forced into abeyance for the 1918/19 season. Problems of transport had seen them leave the Scottish League in 1917 to play in a hastily arranged Eastern Division, but even that had collapsed in 1918/19, and other than for the occasional friendly or an Army game, Dens Park was closed 'for the duration' or 'until better days'.

Better days did come in August 1919 when football started again. Yet a glance at the files of *The Courier* for summer 1919 will show that Britain (and the world) was a far from settled place. Dreadful conflicts continued in Ireland and Russia. In Britain itself, sporadic strikes in the mines, on the railways, rent strikes in Glasgow and in Rosyth, Fife, all played havoc. Worse still was what happened in Liverpool in 1919, when the police went on strike. Such was the ensuing lawlessness that the city had to be placed under martial law and the Riot Act was read at Birkenhead. This gave the military the power to shoot anyone who did not instantly obey instructions. On one occasion, shots had to be fired over the heads of looters.

But locally, there were clear signs that life was returning to normal when the Forfar Games were held on 28 July 1919 at Station Park (and Carseview Park, the new home of East End Football Club, at the back of Station Park), under the tutelage of Forfar Athletic Football Club for the first time. It was, by all accounts, an emotional and drunken celebration, but a totally peaceful occasion. Troup had, of course, kept himself fit during the war, playing for various regimental teams. He also trained hard during the summer of 1919 – such was his enthusiasm to get back into the game – and, of course, he was still a contracted player for Dundee. The first game at Dens Park was the public trial on 13 August, when Troup played for the Reds against the Blues, along with another two Forfarians, George Henderson and Dyken Nicoll.

Dundee's first real game was away to Motherwell – a game that they lost 1-3. This was 'hardly surprising' according to *The Courier*, 'in view of the fact that Motherwell had played together during the entire war' – an unkind dig at perceived war dodging, presumably. *The Courier* was very proud of one of Dundee's new recruit, one Davie Raitt from Buckhaven Victoria, possessor of the Military Medal for Gallantry. Davie had also been an intructor in Physical Education while in the forces. He and Alec very soon became close friends.

The following week, for the first home game, Troup was back in his erstwhile place on the Dens Park left wing, as Third Lanark went down 1-3 to a strong Dundee team. Troup, being one of the ex-servicemen, received a special cheer. He would have appreciated that, but must have been distressed at the sight of the number of men wearing the 'hospital blue' uniform in their special enclosure. These were the maimed and the injured of the Black Watch, the Royal Flying Corps (or Royal Air Force, as it was now called) or even Troup's own Royal Engineers. Such wounded ex-Servicemen were allowed into games free of charge.

There was something ironically appropriate about Dundee's first game after the First World War being against Third Lanark. Third Lanark, who went to the wall in 1967 following at least a decade of mismanagement, corruption and blatant embezzlement, were actually formed as an army regiment team called The 3rd Lanark Rifle Volunteers. Even by 1919, any great connection with the military had disappeared, but they were still nicknamed 'The Sodgers'.

Troup, as he ran up and down his left wing, may have been surprised to hear a man in the crowd with a stentorian voice giving a commentary on the action. ' ... Troup running up the wing, a short pass inside to Willie Brown, but cut out by a red shirt of Third Lanark, and the ball is now ... ' It would be a good ten years before the wireless would be able to give a commentary to the general public, but this new phenomenon was a man describing the action to about twenty men with bandages over their eyes or wearing dark glasses. They were the war-blinded.

Outside the ground, a feature of attendance at football matches in these days was the proliferation of beggars. Some would sing Scottish songs or current favourites like 'Home in Pasadena' (the current favourite for returning US troops) or a few Irish songs (if Celtic or Hibs were playing); others would simply stand on their one leg with a placard which said 'Woonded (sic) at Somme' while an ill-dressed, runny-nosed little girl would hold out a cap for a few pennies. Older girls would, with a nod and wink, ply their none-too-subtle trade – and all in all, Dundee in the immediate post-war years was anything but 'the land fit for heroes to live in', of which Lloyd George boasted.

There was one song, however, which might risk arrest if sung. This was the socialist anthem 'The Red Flag'.

> The people's flag is deepest red
> It shrouded oft our martyred dead
> But ere their limbs grew stiff and cold
> Their blood had drenched its every fold
>
> Then lift the scarlet banner high!
> Beneath its fold we fight and die!
> Let traitors mock and cowards sneer!
> We'll keep the Red Flag flying here!

This song was much disapproved of by the Establishment in 1919 and 1920. Everyone knew that there had been a Red Revolution in Russia (indeed British troops were still in action supporting the ill-fated counter-revolution of the White Russians) and the Establishment were terrified of it happening in Britain. Such a revolution might well have happened in defeated Germany had not the victorious Allies imposed upon the Germans the (fundamentally weak) Weimar Republic. Closer to home, there had been a strong Socialist element in the Irish rebellion of 1916, which the British were still subduing at the cost of much bloodshed, and even closer still, the riots of January 1919 in George Square, Glasgow, had terrified those who feared a more equal sharing of wealth.

For these reasons, the 'Red Flag' song was not permitted. So what did football fans do about it? It was a very catchy tune and imaginative lyrics were found. They involved Celtic's legendary goalkeeper Charlie Shaw, of whom many stories had spread during Celtic's predominant years of the First World War. Charlie, for example, would get so bored that he would go home for his tea or wander round to the other goal and ask the other goalkeeper if he needed any help. Few people scored against Charlie, so when they did it was a great event. Nobody knows which set of supporters started this particular song, although there is a certain amount of evidence to suggest that it was John 'Tokey' Duncan of Raith Rovers who scored the famous goal. It became immortalised in Rangers legend about Alan Morton, but Dundee fans always sang:

> Oh, Charlie Shaw, he never saw
> Far oor wee Troupie pit the ba'

He pit the ba' richt in the net
And Charlie Shaw sat doon and gret!

Oh, Charlie Shaw, he asked his ma'
Far oor wee Troupie pit the ba'
His mither said 'Just up ye get
And stop lying there in the wet!'

And poor McNair was in despair
For Troup was here and Troup was there
But that day he'll no' forget
How oor wee Troupie found the net

Many verses were added, not all of them repeatable, but one referred to Lochee-born John Bell, Dundee's centre forward:

Oh, Johnnie Bell went through hi'sel
And cawed puir Charlie a tae hell
Then Troupie cam an saw the ba'
And put anither by Charlie Shaw!

The activity of Johnnie Bell refers to the now grossly illegal 'shoulder charging' on the goalkeeper – a tactic that amazingly survived in British football until the 1950s, until it was publicly seen for what it was in the FA Cup finals of 1957 and 1958 and, under European influence, gradually disappeared.

Another song about the same 'goal' was put to the tune of 'After the ball was over' – a bawdy song made popular by soldiers in the war.

After the ball was centred,
After the whistle blew,
Rawlings got up his temper (sic)
And down the wing he flew
He passed the ball to Troupie
And Troupie scored a goal
That was one for Dundee
And Celtic were up the pole!

It is a shame when facts get in the way of a good story, but sadly for Dundee fans, Alec Troup never in fact managed to score a goal against Charlie Shaw of Celtic. Old men would win themselves free drinks in Dundee hostelries as late at the 1970s and 1980s by telling everyone that they were there when 'Troupie' cut inside, dribbled round about eight Celtic defenders and shot past Charlie from ten, twelve, twenty or even thirty yards ... but sadly it never happened. Norrie Price's *They Wore The Dark Blue* – an excellent and comprehensive account of every Dundee game – can find

*Alec Troup, Dundee, c. 1919.*

no mention of a Troup goal scored against Charlie Shaw.

This creation of a legendary but fictitious goal, however, does tell us a great deal about Alec Troup. In an age which badly needed a hero and a legend, why does Dundee folk culture latch itself onto Alec Troup as the man who beat Charlie Shaw? Simply, because the Forfarian was the Dundee hero of the time. The wee, insignificant looking but clean-cut, morally honest and thoroughly likeable man was the man that the downtrodden people of the jute mills looked to as an example someone who had had 'deliverance' from boring, monotonous jobs.

And being small meant that he was one of them. It was the same thing which explained the popularity of Charlie Chaplin in the silent cinema. Dundee people identified with the small man whom they subliminally viewed as being like them, distinct from the fat, bullying jute barons. Not only that, but his dapper, clean-cut appearance and blameless lifestyle mean that Troup was the sort of man they would aspire to be. He had served his country. He was a brilliant player. He was a good role model.

In truth, there was a great deal to be happy with as far as Troup's form was concerned. Consistently, newspapers sang his praises. Both the Dundee papers, *The Courier* and *The Advertiser,* talked highly of him, although occasionally an 'opposition' newspaper like Kirkcaldy's *Fife Free Press* would report equally favourably on him. This article was about a 3-1 Dundee victory at Stark's Park on 15 November 1919: 'Troup was the finest winger that has kicked a ball in Kirkcaldy this season, and his partner, Slade, was a good runner-up in push and go.'

Dundee's supporters were generally pleased with their team, who finished fourth in the League in 1920. Troup had had a magnificent season, but there had also been much to cheer the Dundonians in the play of full-backs Davie Raitt and Napper Thomson, centre half Dyken Nicoll (like Troup, a Forfarian,) and Johnny Bell's 28 goals had also been a source of much joy. In Donald Slade, Troup had an ideal left-wing partner, and of course, Troup's international cap against England (detailed in a later chapter) had also been a great moment for his many fans.

The best game for entertainment value had been the 7-1 demolition of hapless Ayr

United on 29 November 1919, but the most significant performance came on 24 January when Dundee beat Airdrie 1-0 in the Scottish Cup. Troup was outrageously treated by the Airdrie defenders but showed 'how trickery could be made profitable'. It was, however, a very profitable experience for Dundee, for they now had Celtic at home in the Scottish Cup.

Funnily enough, Celtic would now come to Dens Park two weeks in a row, on League business on 31 January, then the Scottish Cup on 7 February. Dundee won the League game 2-1, to set alight an already frenzied Tayside for the Scottish Cup game. The war was now well and truly over, and life and football were back! The newspapers can but give a flavour of the expectations created about the game and the phrase 'the roaring twenties' might have been coined with this match and its pre-match hype in mind. Mr Winston Churchill, for example, the sitting MP, was due to have a political meeting on 7 February to talk about things like 'free trade' and 'coal' and 'international relationships' but wisely cancelled it, because he realised that he would have to play second fiddle to the Dundee *v.* Celtic match.

Both teams went into retreat. Dundee took their players to Edzell for the intervening week where they trained, played golf, went for walks, allowed the press to take photographs of them, and discussed tactics. Celtic, similarly, did not return to Glasgow after the League game, but took up residence at the Bruce Hotel, Carnoustie where Willie Maley, 'the genial manager', gave interviews, charmed the local populace and invited everyone to join the Celtic team at a soirée, where everyone was invited to do a party piece of a song, a recitation or a conjuring or juggling performance! There was also, of course, the serious business of training for the very important Cup tie.

CELTIC.

A. McNAIR.

Both Dundee newspapers built up the atmosphere for the Saturday, talking about the amount of 'brake-clubs' and charabancs that would arrive from the west, 'blowing bugles and banging drums', and the number of Dundee supporters who would arrive from their hinterland of Forfar, Brechin and Arbroath. The game is previewed in a series of articles by Abner T. Lyall, who thought that Napper Thomson would nullify the menace of Andy McAtee; that the 'boy wonder' Tommy McInally would make no impression on Dyken

*Alec McNair of Celtic, a doughty opponent and a close friend of Troup. McNair saved Alec from serious injury in a riot at Parkhead in 1920. He later became manager of Dundee.*

*Dundee FC, 1920. From left to right: Philip, Jackson, Bell, Thomson, Raith, Troup.*

Nicoll; and that Celtic's goalkeeper, Charlie Shaw, would have problems keeping out McLaughlin and Bell. He was worried about the great Jimmy McMenemy, however, but thought that Dundee had the players to deal with him. He said '... and that younker (sic) Troup is the star compendium of tricks. In the words of the warbler "He's little, he's wise, he's a terror for his size", and he's never on the same spot twice. When the big chap against him is handing out the biff mixture, Troup does the vanishing biz, but he would be well advised not to beat the same man twice. Better to beat two men once ...'

The day of the game was bright and breezy, and a crowd of about 35,000, according to some sources, shoehorned into the grossly inadequate Dens Park to see a great game – but it turned out to be disappointing and unfortunate for Dundee. Adam McLean, Celtic's left winger, took advantage of a moment's hesitation in the first minute to put Celtic ahead, and even worse followed when Dyken Nicoll, 'the Lion Heart' (as *The Courier* calls him), was carried off quarter of an hour later. This was before the days of substitutes, and Dundee were down to ten men.

A feature of the game was the joust between Troup and his good friend Alec McNair. Honours were even in the first half, but as Celtic, with McMenemy outstanding, took command in the second half with goals from McInally and Cringan, Troup was starved of the ball. He was 'keen, clever, thrustful and pining for passes which never came', until, late in the game, he evaded McNair and crossed for Jim McLaughlan to score a late consolation goal for Dundee.

McNair, who would one day became manager of Dundee, was, according to the *Dundee Advertiser*, 'more effective and more gentlemanly than others. Great as Troup is, he may now know that some of the tricks which outwit nine defenders in ten have no effect on Alec McNair'. But Troup was still learning. He was only twenty-five, not yet at his peak, despite having lost some of his best years to the war, and the time was fast approaching when nobody would get the better of him.

If there was a down side to Troup, it was that he was always suffering recurrent problems with his shoulder and collarbone. Even heavy strapping was not always adequate protection against a bad fall. On 11 October 1919, in a game against Dumbarton at Boghead (often called 'fatal Boghead' from the days when Celtic and Rangers would be lucky to escape with a draw – and in this case it was almost fatal to a fine career) Troup was playing well and Dundee were well on top of Dumbarton, whom they eventually beat 3-0. He got possession of the ball and sped down the wing. He lost control of the ball. He caught up with it and in one movement tried to turn and hit it over into the middle. He overbalanced, threw out an arm to save himself, and the next minute felt a strange and painful sensation – as if his arm had been cut off. On this occasion, Troup needed a doctor to put the dislocated shoulder back into position.

On 13 December 1919, a couple of months later, in a great game against Raith Rovers at Dens Park which finished 5-4 for Dundee, Troup fell heavily and everyone suspected a broken collarbone. He was carried off, but the shoulder was once again only dislocated and Troup returned after five minutes to a tremendous cheer from the 10,000 fans. It was Troup who fed Slade to score the two crucial goals in the second half.

In time, Troup would realise that there was no cure. It was a genetic condition which his great-grandson suffers from today, and he soon learned how to right his shoulder himself if it ever happened again. Sometimes he could massage it back into position. Other times, he would just lie down and give himself a twist! And, for preventative measures, he would wrap even more bandages round himself before the start of a game.

The 1919/20 season saw Troup's first Scottish cap, but Troup also had a terrifying experience of crowd trouble before the end of the season. As luck would have it, Dundee had to travel to Glasgow twice on the April holiday weekend to play both members of the Old Firm – Rangers at Ibrox on Saturday 24 April and Celtic at

*Dundee FC, 1919/20. Note the obvious insertion of Dave Hutcheson (fourth from left, back row), who has a huge head and body – but no feet! From left to right, back row: Raitt, Thomson, Watson, Hutcheson, Nicoll, McIntosh, Downie, Orr, Ferguson, Langair (trainer). Front row: Rawlings, McLaughlan, Bell, Slade, Troup, Buchan.*

Parkhead on Monday 26 April. The climax to the League title was close between the two Glasgow teams, and although Rangers were marginally ahead, Dundee would have a large say in where the Championship went.

Sadly, Dundee chose to put on their worst performance of the season at Ibrox and went down 1-6. The defence had a nightmare, losing four goals before half-time against the wind, and Troup, although instrumental in Slade's solitary counter, had been unable to do much against a well-drilled and determined Rangers defence. It was, in fact, a disgraceful display from a Dundee team who would finish fourth in the League, and some of the players did themselves few favours by saying that Rangers were a fine team and would be 'worthy champions'.

The Dundee press were strongly disapproving of both the performance and the apparent grovelling to Rangers. 'It would be foolish to construct excuses, for Dundee were outclassed and outplayed' is how *The Courier* puts it. Nicoll was 'off-colour', Jackson was 'poor' and McIntosh 'only fair'. 'All eyes were on Troup but for once in a while he was under a cloud', and the rest of the forward line 'availed nothing'. It was quite simply a poor performance.

The Celtic fans saw it somewhat differently and put an even worse interpretation on these events. They claimed that there had been some bribery or that there was a Protestant conspiracy to keep Celtic from winning the League, and that Dundee had 'co-operated' with Rangers. Ireland at the time was in uproar as the Black and Tans carried out their pogrom of Republican sympathisers, and Celtic fans, some of whom were Sinn Fein supporters, saw this as an extension of British imperialism's evil rule.

The Celtic club, of course, did not share (at least not publicly) this interpretation of events, but that Sunday, the East End of Glasgow seethed with rumours and gossip. Dundee's players, in the meantime, had been told in no uncertain terms by manager Sandy MacFarlane that they would have to raise their game against Celtic, for there was no excuse for such a spineless performance. They were reminded that the contracts for next season would soon be given out, and that there must be no repeat of such a display when the other half of the Old Firm were met on Monday at Parkhead.

In such a poisonous atmosphere with Dundee, (eccentrically and inexplicably wearing red jerseys – perhaps an attempt to deflect some hatred associated with wearing a blue jersey) were booed onto the park by a none-too-numerous, but none-theless nasty Celtic crowd. There were about 7,000 present – the rest having presum-ably given up for the season, although there was still a theoretical chance of the Championship – and Dundee soon realised that they would have a fight on their hands. Celtic (even although they lacked their genius Patsy Gallacher) fired on all cylinders, and Dundee defenders like Dyken Nicoll, Davie Raitt and Napper Thomson were forced to tackle 'fairly robustly', as their apologists would put it. The robust tackling was not all one-sided, however, for both Jackson and Bell sustained injuries.

On the playing side, Celtic were clearly the better team, but bad finishing let them down. Late in the second half, with the score at 1-1 (Troup having fed Slade to equalise a Willie McStay penalty), Dundee were defending desperately. Right winger Archie Rawlings, playing as a double right-back, as it were, against Celtic's talented Adam McLean, committed a reckless tackle on the said Adam, with Bert

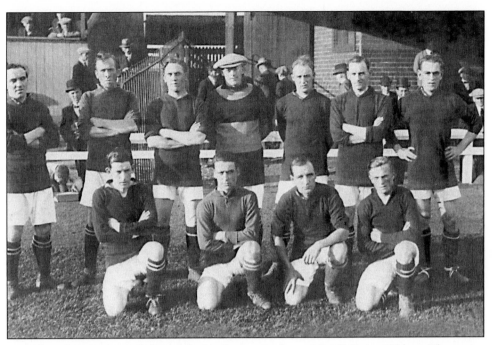

*Dundee, 1920/21. From left to right, back row: Jackson, Nicoll, Raitt, Gibbon, Thomson, Philip, Irving. Front row: McDonald, Bell, Slade, Troup. Observe the middle-class, genteel clientele in the background – bow ties, bowler hats and dark suits.*

McIntosh in attendance as well. McLean then appeared to lash out at McIntosh but missed and collapsed to nurse his injuries. Rawlings was actually lucky not to be sent off, but it was his apparent swaggering refusal to enquire about McLean's health that caused the trouble.

One hothead jumped over the low perimeter wall (the railings had been removed to help the war effort in 1915 and had not yet been replaced), and he was soon followed by about twenty others, initially eight- to fourteen-year-old boys, but then older elements, who should have had more sense, used the opportunity to vent their frustration and hate on the Dundee players. Bert McIntosh and Davie Raitt were both viciously attacked, and the diminutive Troup would have been as well, had it not been for his proximity to his rival and friend Alec McNair. McNair and McStay bravely stemmed the tide of attackers to allow the Dundee players to reach the security of the pavilion in the corner of the ground.

The game was thus abandoned with some time yet left to play. The authorities decided that the result would stand as 1-1, and Parkhead was to be closed for a spell. *The Courier* was outraged at this, and so was all of Scottish football, and Celtic lapsed into embarrassed silence. For Troup and the other Dundee players, it was a salutary reminder of how fine a line there was between support for a team and mob hysteria, given the lethal cocktail of perceived injustice, an uneasy political situation and the aftermath of a dreadful war where young men had learned, all too successfully, how to be violent.

The Celtic and Dundee teams themselves, who had hitherto enjoyed a friendly, albeit competitive relationship, made every effort to make things up. Celtic had some time previously agreed to play a friendly at Dens Park on 4 May in aid of the St Patrick's War Memorial Fund in Dundee (St Patrick's being a local Catholic church). A total of 15,000 spectators turned up on a fine night to see a vigorous but fairly-contested friendly.

Troup felt sufficiently confident about his own abilities (particularly in view of his international appearance in April 1920) that he held out against re-signing for the following season until better terms were offered. Rumour had it that several clubs made enquiries about him – Newcastle, Sunderland and even Rangers were reputed to be interested, before turning their attention to Queen's Park's Alan Morton. Troup probably had no great desire to leave Dundee at this point and very soon came to terms with his club.

The season of 1920/21 saw Dundee once again fourth in the Scottish League. Troup was an ever-present, apart from the times when he was involved in international duty. This year, however, there was more of a problem finding a good left-wing partner for Alec. No fewer than eight were tried following the departure from the scene of Donald Slade, but there was no permanent success. Slade's disappearance from the scene is a mystery, for Troup and he had always got on well together. But Slade was held responsible for a defeat at Hamilton on 8 September, was dropped to the reserves to be replaced by George Philip, and never reappeared. It is no exaggeration to say that if Dundee's forward line had all played with the consistency and tenacity of Alec Troup, the League Championship could have been won.

Certainly attendances were high with the average well above 15,000 and Troup was now a cult hero.

> 'Oh my darling, oh my darling, oh my darling Eckie Troup
> Comes from Forfar, bonnie Forfar, he's my darling Eckie Troup'

This ditty clearly lacked both inspiration and originality, but once again is an indication of how much he was loved by the Dundee supporters. It is important, too, at this point, to remark how vital a thing football was in the lives of working people. Nobody could ever say that there is any lack of public interest in football now, eighty years down the line, but it was even more obsessive and all-encompassing then, for the simple reason that, with cinema in its infancy, radio not yet with them and television over thirty years away, football was virtually all there was. And there was a real need for a form of escapism in the early 1920s.

Crowds, according to the newspaper pictures, were at least ninety-five per cent male, but well-dressed ones. Collar and tie were very much in evidence, and everyone wore a bonnet, whatever the weather! But they were not always as well behaved as they would seem. The sad incident at Celtic Park in April 1920 was by no means an isolated phenomenon. James E. Handley, for example, writer of *The Celtic Story*, spent a large amount of his working life as a priest in Dundee. Here, he is talking about 1920s crowds in general as he bemoans the prevalence of bad language.

> Gross language is not an unusual kind of safety-valve for the untutored urban Scot in his rare moments of emotion; but the war, among its other evils had popularised that type of vocabulary for the common man who had fought overseas or had worked in the munitions factories and shipyards; and the vogue of coupon-filling, together with the introduction of half-time-scoreboards, provided emotional outlets for such kind of expressiveness among the rabble followers of football in the post-war age. The evil and bitterness have become intensified. Any 'needle' game will crowd the terracing with decent men who have come to enjoy the encounter, but weaving through their ranks is the pack of morons on the prowl for whatever will excite their spleen and allow them to voice their disapproval in the limited, repetitive vocabulary of the coarsely subnormal.

Strong stuff indeed, but not entirely without justification. The writer from *The Courier* was saddened by what he witnessed at the Dundee *v.* Kilmarnock game on 30 October 1920, when two bottles were thrown at referee Mr Kelso. Fortunately, no one was injured, but the reporter, although admitting that he was not entirely in agreement with quite a few of Mr Kelso's decisions either, stresses that there is no place in Dundee for such hooliganism.

Indeed, the danger would have been one of a public lynching of the culprits, had either of these two bottles come anywhere near Dundee's star man. The game against Kilmarnock (the holders of the Scottish Cup) ended in a fine 3-1 victory for the Dens Park side. According to *The Courier* writer, 'Troup provided the best incident of the game. A cross from the right came to the outside left, some fifteen yards from goal and, taking deliberate aim, he drove a low ball into the net with terrific force, Hillcoat (Kilmarnock's goalkeeper) touching it, but failing to stay its progress at the base of the right-hand post. Troup showed what he is capable of when the ball is passed to him in the manner in which the winger is entitled to expect it.'

It was not all rosy, however, that season, for the week after that, Dundee went to Ibrox and lost 0-5. Dundee were booed by the Rangers crowd, for some of their tackling was 'strenuous' – (a 1920s euphemism, one feels, for dirty) and Troup, although the only Dundee forward to threaten the Ibrox defence, 'showed an inclination to square the ball prematurely.' And just to show that not all Forfarians played for Dundee, four of Rangers' five goals that day were scored by George Henderson, a Forfarian friend and associate of Troup.

And there were times when the writers of *The Courier* had to upbraid the other players of Dundee for their lack of service to 'Eckie'. On 20 November 1920, Dundee lost 0-2 to Hibs at Easter Road. 'The little winger dazzled when he

*Dens Park, 27 August 1921. Dundee 2, Third Lanark 0. Note the large crowd (17,000) and the almost-completed North Stand. The old North Stand was soon to be demolished – this was possibly its last match day. Here, Third Lanark are on the attack but the ball was to go past the post.*

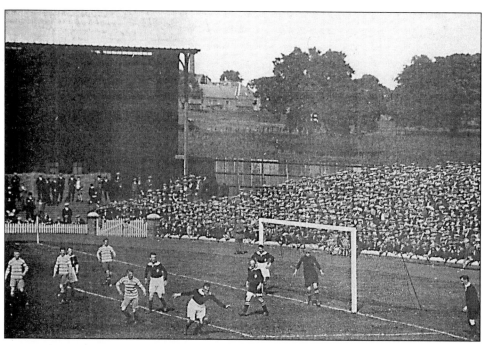

*A magnificent picture of Dens Park, Dundee, in the 1920s. Note the number of 'doolichter' bonnets, the wearing of which was almost universal among adult males. Dundee are pictured defending a Morton corner.*

**SOME OF THE 15,000 SPECTATORS AT DENS PARK**

*The crowd at Dens Park on a cold day in 1921. Observe the two soldiers in the crowd and the universality of hats.*

did get the ball and under these circumstances it is passing strange that he was practically ignored at times. Troup had to resort to individualism to get towards the Edinburgh citadel.'

After the New Year in 1921, Dundee, having disposed of minor opposition, had a prolonged battle against Aberdeen in the third round of the Scottish Cup. It took them three attempts to win through. The first game was on 19 February at Dens Park before a large 27,000 crowd who were disappointed to see a goal-less draw. Wednesday afternoon at Pittodrie saw another draw, this time Dundee being indebted to an own goal by Aberdeen's big Jock Hutton (who would one day play alongside Troup for Scotland) to keep them in the competition. Ibrox – incredibly for a tussle between Dundee and Aberdeen – was the venue for the second replay on 1 March before 15,000, and it was Alec Troup who confirmed the victory. Already one up and with time running out for the Dons, Troup picked up a ball about twenty-five yards from goal. He took a couple of steps, steadied himself and as several defenders converged, fired into the far corner of the net. Dundee were thus into the quarter-final and hopes were high for the Scottish Cup.

Their opponents were Albion Rovers on 5 March at Dens Park. This game was a huge disappointment to the 15,000 fans who were there; the 2-0 victory for Albion Rovers was a shock, but not necessarily a huge one. In 1921, the Coatbridge outfit were good Cup fighters and indeed had contested last season's Scottish Cup final. The supine manner of the defeat caused distress among the Dens Park faithful, however. Troup was 'insufficiently supported' and seldom took the eye.

*The Courier* on the Monday was almost in mourning. It had not been a good weekend for the Tories or for Dundee FC. Thoroughly alarmed by the victory of Labour

*Alec and Dave McDonald are not about to do the Highland fling. They are merely having a break from training, sometime during the early 1920s.*

candidate Tom Kennedy in a by-election in Kirkcaldy and fearing for the future of western civilisation, the leader writer launches into an attack on contemporary social morality, claiming that the war had led to 'lawlessness and licence', women wearing

*Dens Park, September 1921. The new North Stand is just about completed. The wooden South Stand in the foreground, rotten and a safety hazard, mysteriously caught on fire that Christmas Eve.*

lipstick – and the desperately awful performance of Dundee FC, who had wasted 'all their good work hitherto this season'.

Thereafter, Dundee did what was necessary to keep their fans happy, namely win at home. Away form wasn't necessarily as good, but the team finished fourth (the same as the previous season), one point below Hearts, although a long way adrift of Rangers and Celtic. Partick Thistle won the Scottish Cup that year, the one and only time that they have done so to date – a fact that increased the frustration on Tayside, for Dundee had beaten Thistle at Dens Park in a League match a week after the Albion Rovers flop.

Troup was now a personality figure in Dundee, but it certainly did not go to his head. He travelled by rail from Forfar every day for training, and he could be seen walking the half mile or so from Dundee East Station to Dens Park in his raincoat, bonnet and carrying a portmanteau with his boots. He was recognised of course, but this did not seem to bother him. He talked to everybody, discussed games, talked to fellow passengers about general matters in the world of football as the train chugged its way to Forfar, passing through places like Monikie, Kirkbuddo and Kingsmuir. It is often said that a football man need never be bored; nor need he be interested in anything else. So it was with Eckie.

The season of 1921/22 saw Dundee yet again come fourth in the League. Celtic won it, Rangers were second and amazingly it was Raith Rovers, with their fine team which included the brilliant half-back line of Raeburn, Morris and Collier as well as the Duncan brothers in the forward line, which came third. Dundee, in fact, could have done a lot better had they been better travellers. They were unbeaten at Dens, with both Rangers and Celtic lucky to get off with goal-less draws; yet they managed to lose 12 times away from home.

Dens Park, indeed, was a heady place to be in those days. Gates were high (although not quite as high as an ambitious club needed) and the ground received a major face lift in the shape of a fine new stand (still in existence today) with its distinctive obtuse angle, designed to give everyone a good view of the game. It was opened in September 1921 before a game with Ayr United in which Troup, returning from an injury, performed meritoriously before all the dignitaries and bigwigs who were present.

Troup had another fine season. His goalscoring was less noticeable, but he laid on many of centre forward Davie Halliday's 23 goals. He also benefited from having a regular inside left. Walter Bird, after an uncertain start, had emerged as a fine player. On 3 October, for example, in the Monday holiday game against Motherwell which ended up in a disappointing 1-1 draw, 'only Troup shaped like pulling the match out of the fire and he was none too liberally supported by Bird', but by the end of the season *The Courier* was reporting that 'the left-wing pairing of Bird and Troup have few equals in the modern game' as well as making a few weak puns about Bird 'twittering away cheerily' to Troup.

Only two full-backs seemed able to prevent Troup from showing his mettle. One was Celtic's Alec McNair, Troup's old adversary for many years now. The highlight of a 0-0 draw when Celtic came to Dens Park on 8 October was the 'thrilling encounter' between the two of them, after which neither was able to claim 'total victory' and both came off the field arm in arm. What people liked about Troup *v.* McNair was that it was real football in both cases – no fouling, no mouthing at the referee and no snarling at each other.

A lot less gentlemanly was Paddy Crossan of Hearts. On 15 October at Tynecastle, Crossan, 'with a style that would frighten a ghost', clashed badly with Troup. Troup did not retaliate, but played no significant part in the game thereafter, and Crossan was spoken to by the referee when sterner measures seemed to be called for. Dundee, in fact, did rather well to earn a draw that day, considering that their half-back, Sam Irving, who would eventually be capped for Ireland, collapsed at Tay Bridge Station before they left Dundee with a bout of malaria! This particular disease was normally not too common in Dundee in October, it has to be said, but poor Sam had caught it while fighting at Salonika in the First World War, and it was a recurrent condition.

On Christmas Eve in 1921, not long after the spectators left Dens Park after seeing Troup inspire Dundee to a 2-0 win over Hamilton, an untoward and possibly providential thing happened. With the opening of the palatial North Stand, the old wooden South one, rotten with woodworm and dry rot and which was to be demolished at the end of the season, was now redundant. Indeed, it had served the club very well for it had been carried stick by stick from Dundee's previous home at Carolina Port in 1899 and re-assembled lovingly at Dens Park.

But it had now seen better days. The dressing room and the administrative area were to be moved to the North Stand. Then, lo and behold, the South Stand caught fire, lighting up the northern part of the city in the same way that a star had lit up Bethlehem on a previous Christmas Eve. *The Courier* does not quite repeat the commonly-held local belief that this was deliberate arson on the part of the directors, but does state succinctly that this was a 'singular coincidence' and adds caustically and perhaps cynically, 'It was insured!'

Norrie Price's excellent *Up Wi' The Bonnets* is similarly unimpressed with the idea that the fire was an act of God. He tells the story of Jimmy Guthrie who played for Dundee ten years later. Jimmy used to say that on three previous occasions this obsolete structure had caught on fire but a conscientious groundsman (clearly not privy to the inner machinations) had on each occasion doused the flames. He was eventually sacked. Dare we use the word 'fired'?

Such mildly outrageous behaviour on the part of their management had absolutely no effect on the players who were at Ibrox on Boxing Day for a game which they had to win if a Championship challenge was to be maintained. The weather was poor, and of course Boxing Day in 1921 was not a holiday for everyone, so the attendance was cut to a very disappointing 12,000. They saw a dismal game, which Rangers won 2-1, the highlight for Dundee being Troup's goal when he outwitted Manderson and slammed the ball into the far corner. The national press were in surprising unanimity about the fact that Troup had a better game against Manderson than Alan Morton did against his direct opponent Davie Raitt. *The Courier* laboured this point somewhat to press Troup's claim for Scottish caps, but was disappointed with the general Dundee performance.

1922 opened brightly with a win over Aberdeen at the New Year, but again the team lacked the ability to win consistently, too many games which might have been won becoming draws. Dundee were an attractive team to watch, but did seem to lack the killer instinct. Troup was still consistently good, but suffered a setback in January. He played in the game at Dens Park on 14 January. This was against Morton – a game that Dundee won on a snow-clad landscape by 2-1. Troup had a good first half, but

significantly 'didn't maintain his brilliance in the second half'. He was slowing down, had a sore throat, his legs were heavy and Troup knew instantly what the problem was, (for he had suffered previously, mildly it has to be said, but had also observed it in others) – it was flu.

The newspapers in early 1922 were all full of advice about gargling and taking tablets to avoid a recurrence of the influenza virus which was all too similar to the horror of 1918 and 1919, the so-called 'Spanish flu'. World-wide, this

*Troup in action in a game against Hibs in January 1922 at Dens Park.*

*Troup was absent with influenza in the early months of 1922. But Dundee still beat Queen's Park 3-0!*

*A cigarette card of Alec Troup. Collecting these cards was a popular hobby in the 1920s.*

F.&J. SMITH'S CIGARETTES

DUNDEE.

A TROUP.

virus probably killed more people than the trenches did – an ambitious claim but apparently true, and epidemiologists thought that this 1922 version was the same one back for a second attempt on the general population. As the war was now well and truly over and some sort of medical services were now available, this particular epidemic was less serious, but still had an effect.

Diseases will thrive when conditions are poor, as any student of the modern-day Third World will tell you. In Dundee with its slums, overcrowded and teeming with humanity – in many cases uneducated humanity bred, it would appear, as factory fodder, evil prevailed. Even fit and healthy people like professional footballers, with their comparatively salubrious lifestyles, were not immune once the germ had taken a hold of the general population.

In Troup's case, it was quite simply off home to Forfar and bed, to be cared for by mother Christina, sister Jane and visited by girlfriend Elizabeth. In fact, it was Jane who was now running the house, for Christina's dementia, which had been apparent for some time, was now getting worse. She still retained her good humour and loveable character, and could occasionally be quite lucid and sharp – but needed more or less constant nursing and attention. She couldn't be left on her own, for she might do strange and dangerous things.

Alec's flu meant that he missed three games and, perhaps importantly, ruined the chance that he might have been considered for the Scotland game against Wales in Wrexham on 4 February. He returned on 11 February to play at Larkhall against Larkhall Royal Albert in the Scottish Cup. These were no easy opponents, and Alec was 'closely attended' by several defenders. This did release some of the pressure off Davie Halliday, though, and it was Halliday who scored the only goal of the game. A promising Cup run, however, was brought to a shuddering halt by an appalling defensive performance at Pittodrie at the end of February which saw the Aberdeen men win 3-0 – and it should have been more.

Fourth place was thus Dundee's lot, behind champions Celtic, Rangers and Raith Rovers. The Kirkcaldy men had done well (their best ever season) and yet Dundee came close to catching them. Indeed, Dundee beat them 1-0 at Dens Park on 19 April

The malignant Gods of Ill-chance seemed to "have it in for" Dundee on Saturday. Sooner did a strong man rise in the Dark Blue ranks than he was smitten hip thigh, or elsewhere.

Thus Nicol who, bringing off one of his celebrated headers, volplaned violently into an opponent

Then fell poor Napper Thomson followed by — his partner Raitt

('Tis whispered that, following the example of the Italian Government in buying the larynx of Caruso, the Town of Forfar intend purchasing the frontal bone of Nicol.)

*25 February 1922. Dundee crash out of the Scottish Cup 0-3 to Aberdeen at Pittodrie, in a rough match. Some indication is given of the rough treatment meted out to Troup by Aberdeen's big Jock Hutton – a Scottish international colleague of Troup's.*

when Troup created the only goal of the game. He broke away on the wing, showing a turn of speed (for which he was not always famed) and sent over a cross to Davie Halliday. Halliday's shot was saved by Raith goalkeeper Brown but Willie Cowan was on hand to hammer home the rebound.

There was no lessening in the popularity of Alec Troup, who continued to be the toast of the jute mills. It was probably at this point, as the season came to its end, that Troup may well have begun to wonder whether success might be achieved with another club. It was well known that Dundee were looking for ways of paying off their debt brought about by their new stand and other ground improvements, and would be not averse to a transfer of Troup. But where? Rangers would hardly buy another left-winger if they had Alan Morton, and Celtic, who seldom bought players in those days anyway had the perfectly adequate Adam McLean. Troup would have realised that if he were to go anywhere else, it would have to be England ... but Alec was a home-loving Forfar boy.

The season had not long finished before Alec had the melancholy task of arranging for his mother's funeral. Most of his family were by now abroad and out of Forfar, and Alec and Jane, who had cared for Christina, were now left on their own. In his heart of hearts, however, Alec probably knew that it was for the best, for living with a

—after that it was Fotheringham, the ulti-handed, versus Aberdeen.

Herewith Hutton and Troup - giving some idea of what the game looked like.

er the Aberdeen centre ht have scored a dozen ls, **BUT** ———

Wm. Robertson.

relative whose arteries had hardened due to 'arterial sclerosis', and who suffered from dementia, would wear anyone down. Perhaps Jane could now find herself a man and get married. And what about Alec's love life?

It was progressing, and very soon circumstances would propel it forward irreversibly, but season 1922/23 opened with Dundee having lost Davie Raitt, the right-back from Lochgelly and a good friend of Troup, to Everton. But Dundee had also bought (to Alec's great delight) his fellow Forfarian, the much-travelled Davie McLean. Those who looked askance at the thirty-two-year-old McLean, thinking that he was past his best, were to be proved hideously wrong, for not only did 'Davitt' score 23 goals that season, he also played another three seasons after that for Dundee, even scoring a goal in the 1925 Scottish Cup final. And that is without mentioning the other six seasons he played after that for his beloved Forfar!

In fact, the Forfar pair only played 10 games together for Dundee, because Alec suffered a loss of form in the autumn, necessitating him missing many games. Before then, however, there was a sentimental journey for Alec Troup. Geordie Langlands had been granted a benefit match by Forfar and Dundee were invited to supply the opposition for 'Purkie'. This was 31 August 1922 and 1,500 were at Station Park to see men like Troup and McLean return to their old haunts. Dundee won 4-2 (Troup playing spectacularly well and scoring the third goal) and the crowd showed their appreciation at the end.

Troup was saddened at the beginning of September to hear of the death in a motor-cycle accident of his old adversary, Sunny Jim Young of Celtic. Sunny was, of course, the man who had fouled Troup so mercilessly in 1914 when Troup repeatedly got the better of him, but Sunny was also genial and cheerful. Whenever they met, Sunny would make jokes about his mother and her umbrella, and it was obvious that both men had forgotten and forgiven any nastiness. Indeed, they held each other in high regard.

Dundee's League form was inconsistent throughout September and Troup looked out of touch. An occasional moment of brilliance would be compensated for by long periods of inaction. The team generally, who had come to rely rather too much on Alec, began to suffer as well. The game on 7 October, for instance, a 1-0 win over Ayr United, is described unequivocally by *The Advertiser* as 'boring'. The reporter then goes on to say 'Troup was not up to scratch, and his displays of late have contained little to enthuse over'.

Manager Sandy MacFarlane must have been a reader of *The Advertiser*, for Alec was dropped for the next game and stayed dropped until December, with Halliday doing well on the left wing and the team beginning to play a little better.

Alec, in fact, was not the only famous man out of favour in Dundee at that particular point in history. The 1922 General Election was held on Wednesday 15 November, when the Coalition Government, which had been in power since 1916, went to the country. It had been showing signs of falling apart in any case, and the result was the return of a Conservative Government under Andrew Bonar-Law. This however was of less importance to Dundonians than the local issue.

It concerned Mr Winston Churchill, one of the two sitting MPs and at this point a Liberal. Rightly, history has given this man the credit for saving the western world from Nazism in 1940 and he will undoubtedly remain one of the greatest historical figures of all time. But in 1922 in Dundee, he was none too popular. *The Courier*, always a Conservative paper, attacked him ruthlessly and *The Advertiser*, for all its Liberal tendencies, could not help falling out with him for his drunkenness, (although Churchill himself had once hypocritically and ironically described Dundee as the 'most drunken city in Europe'!) irresponsible ideas and general 'young man about town with loads of money' attitude to life.

The people in Dundee had no great affection for him either. His aristocratic wife, especially as there were local connections with Airlie near Kirriemuir, did not go down too well with the jute workers, and many people remembered all too well that Churchill had been responsible in the First World War for the disaster at Gallipoli, where the Dundee-based Black Watch had sustained heavy and unnecessary casualties. In addition, the repeated tales of how great a hero he had been in the Boer War were now wearing somewhat thin.

Dundee elected two MPs. A strong campaign was waged by Neddy Scrymgeour, a Prohibitionist candidate, who made much of Churchill's fondness for strong drink, and the infant Labour Party had a strong candidate called Morell. Morell had been a pacifist during the First World War and had come to prominence by exposing some massacre of natives in the name of the British Empire in the Congo. Morell commented unfavourably on Clementine Churchill's pearls and extravagant dress sense. Nearby Kirkcaldy now had a Labour MP in Tom Kennedy, and Fife had not noticeably fallen apart, as the Establishment seemed to think would happen under the guidance of a Labour MP! For the first time, the jute workers realised that they could have their own Labour candidate, someone who would unashamedly represent their own interests. The result was that the workers voted for the Labour man and the churchgoers for the Prohibitionist. They were elected and Churchill was out, not even getting any great sympathy vote for his recent appendix operation!

The election of the Labour candidate did not raise too many eyebrows. It was, after all, part of a general trend – it was the fact that Dundee could elect a Prohibitionist simply to get rid of Winston Churchill that shocked the world. Troup must have been amazed. A teetotaller himself and a voter in Forfar (or 'Montrose Burghs', as it was called) rather than Dundee, he must have permitted himself a wry smile as he kept working away at training in order to regain his first-team place.

Churchill thus left Dundee. In public he was gracious, but later said that he hoped the whole place would be 'swept down the bloody Tay'. Ever adaptable, he soon rejoined the Conservative Party, whom he had ratted on previously. A famous Conservative politician, by no means happy to see this maverick back in the Tory ranks, would say 'I have been a member of this party for longer than Mr Churchill ... but not as often!'

Troup's return to favour was somewhat sooner. Two back-to-back defeats in early December, to Raith Rovers and Rangers, led to a clamour and irresistible demand in the press and the jute mills for his recall. He was picked for the game against Alloa on 16 December. *The Advertiser* on the morning of that game was delighted. 'Everyone knows what Troup can do at his best and if he plays up to his real standard, the forward line will gain in thrustfulness and in shooting power'

This was rich, given that *The Advertiser* had done so much to get him dropped in the first place, but their predictions proved to be correct. 14,000 at Dens saw Dundee win 2-1 with goals from Davie McLean and Alec Troup. *The Advertiser* more or less chortled 'I told you so' on the Monday. 'Troup scored the winning goal and did a great deal more to convince the spectators that his rest had restored to him his self-confidence. His tackling had purpose and courage to it and his combination with Cowan was unquestionably the finest in the game.'

Thus Dundee welcomed back its favourite son after his loss of form, but events would now move rather quickly, and his days at Dens Park were numbered.

# 6

# EVERTON

1923 opened quietly on the football front. Dundee were chugging along in their normal fashion, generally winning home games but doing less well away from home. They drew the New Year's Day game at Pittodrie, but then delighted a large holiday crowd on 2 January by defeating Hibs 1-0 at Dens Park. They then lost at Kilmarnock on the following Saturday before thumping a Perthshire team called Vale of Atholl 6-0 in the Scottish Cup on 13 January.

Dundee and Angus, however, were – if one can believe the local press – all thrilled about the engagement in January 1923 of Lady Elizabeth Bowes-Lyon to the Duke of York. The Bowes-Lyons were based at Glamis Castle, some five miles from Forfar and much famed for its mentions in Shakespeare's *Macbeth*. Indeed, the young Elizabeth, born on 4 August 1900 in London but brought up at Glamis Castle, would often describe herself as a Forfarian. She was of course confirmed in the St John's Episcopalian church of Forfar. Twenty years after her marriage to the Duke of York, when Queen of the British Empire, Elizabeth was inspecting some nurses doing a valiant job for the war effort. She stopped before an earnest young lady and asked 'Where do you come from?' The nervous young nurse stammered 'Forfar'. 'Oh', said the Queen, 'So do I!'

This was all very much in the future and, indeed, not even the most enthusiastic or optimistic of Angus royalists could have imagined in their wildest dreams that this engagement was a step towards Elizabeth becoming Queen. The Duke of York ('Bertie' to his friends) was the second son of George V and suffered from nervous problems caused by an inferiority complex. This was because all the attention was focused on his elder brother, David, who would become King (Edward VIII) when his father died. While David played around with eligible young women, Bertie was gauche, awkward and, worst of all, he stammered. It was not going to be easy for the young Elizabeth, but nobody quite knew quite how hard it was going to be.

What might have been predicted rather more easily by politicians was that there would be another war. The punitive attitude of the Allies to the defeated Germans was evident in the editorials and letters to the editors of all newspapers, national and local. The French were preparing to take over the Ruhr industries because the impoverished Germans had defaulted on reparation payments. A few Germans thought that this 'would lead to a war of revenge', but this was ridiculed by the British press, whose government were doing nothing to stay the revengeful French.

Back at Dens Park, such matters were of little immediate concern to the 12,000

Dundonians who had made their way to watch the football on the crisp wintry day of 20 January. The opponents were Hearts, who usually provided a good game. Not today, however. The game was as poor as the 0-0 score-line would suggest, and all that *The Courier* could find to say about Dundee's forward line was that the left wing pair of McDonald and Troup 'combined happily'.

Unbeknown to anyone other than the Dundee directors, however, was the presence of two men in the lovely new North Stand. They had arrived from Liverpool that morning and were Mr W.C. Cuff, a director of Everton FC, and Mr Thomas McIntosh, the manager of that club. Everton were a rich outfit, but they had struggled since the war, quite clearly losing out to Liverpool their city rivals in the League. More recently, the previous Wednesday afternoon in fact, the 'Toffees' (as they were called) had gone out of the FA Cup to Second Division Bradford. Something had to be done.

Everton and Scotsmen had gone well together in the past. John Robertson, Jack Bell and Sandy Young had all been Scots who had done well for the Toffees. It was time for another cross-border raid, as local talent was clearly not doing its job. The Everton delegation had actually arrived to view two possibilities. One was John White of Hearts and the other was Alec Troup of Dundee. White (although also an international player) had a poor game and was immediately discounted, but five minutes after the full-time whistle, Mr McIntosh approached Sandy MacFarlane, his opposite number at Dundee, and offered a sum 'believed to be in the region of £4,000' for Alec Troup.

Alec was enjoying his bath in the palatial dressing room of the new North Stand after the game. He felt that he had done well enough, but the lack of goals was a depressing factor. We will have to work on that, he mused. His thoughts were cut short by the sudden appearance of Sandy MacFarlane who asked him to come along to the Directors' Room when he was out of his bath and dressed. 'Somebody wants to see you.' Alec thought that this must be yet another Dundee jute baron who wanted to meet him or whose son wanted his autograph, and, dressing as carefully and as particularly as he always did, he sauntered along the corridor, whistling happily, nodding to a few Hearts players, the referee and the girls who had made the tea.

It was only when he was introduced to the two Everton men that he realised what he was here for. Mr McIntosh was brief and to the point. A signing-on fee of 'substantial' proportions (later rumoured to be £1,100, although it was probably a lot less than that) and a massive increase in his weekly wage was offered. Dundee were happy, Everton were happy and, as *The Courier* put it on Monday, 'Troup, like Barkis, was willin' (Barkis, of course was the coach driver who assiduously courted Peggoty in Charles Dickens' *David Copperfield,* using the phrase 'Barkis is willin'.)

Alec had few qualms about accepting the deal. He had felt for a while that his career was stagnating and that a move might be a good idea. He had of course lost form for a while in the autumn and had been 'rested' or, less euphemistically, 'dropped' from the Dundee team. The Everton men were kind, co-operative, brisk and business-like. They would fix him up in digs with a Mrs Brown near Goodison Park, and she would expect him on Thursday.

The following Friday he would meet his new team-mates (including his old friend Davie Raitt, who had joined Everton from Dundee six months previously) and he would probably be in the team that would play Stoke City at Victoria Ground next Saturday. There would of course be no lack of Scotsmen at Goodison (nor has there ever been). In addition to Raitt, there would also be the rugged centre half Hunter Hart who had played for Parkhead Juniors and Airdrie before moving south, and in Troup's time more Scots would join the club.

However, Alec was reluctant to leave his home. He had suffered terrible homesickness during the war, but so had everyone else ... and in any case a move to the city of Liverpool to play football with a huge salary was not exactly comparable to the war-time experience! His decision to take the plunge was taken decisively, although reluctantly and with a few reservations.

Alec was asked not to tell anyone about the business until Sunday when the story would be leaked to the *Sunday Post*. His head was reeling as he made his way with Davie McLean in the dark of that cold January night to catch the 6.15 train to Forfar. Nodding as always to all the supporters who greeted them with comments such as 'Herts were some lucky tae get a draw, Eckie' and 'We should hae goat a penalty, Davie', Alec began to wonder if he had made the right decision.

In the confined space of the railway carriage, Alec told McLean. He was delighted for Alec, and proceeded to tell him about his own experiences with English clubs like Sheffield Wednesday, Preston North End and Bradford Park Avenue. Indeed, Davie's younger brother George was still playing for Bradford. Arriving home, Alec told his sister, who was delighted but overwhelmed by the news. She had known it was likely to happen some day, and although recalling the hideous wartime days, she consoled herself by thinking that at least Liverpool was not Flanders.

There was someone else that Alec told that Saturday night as well. This was Elizabeth Kidd, as he walked her home from the 'Gaffie', as the local cinema, The Pavilion, was now known. The romance had been off and on since before the war, but Alec was now convinced she was the girl for him. The move to Everton would mean that something drastic was going to have to happen in his personal life.

When the news broke on Sunday and Monday, it was probably true to say that feelings were divided. The Forfarians were delighted for their favourite player, and many people would come up to him and his sister in the street and wish him all the best. Dundee supporters, on the other hand, felt angry and betrayed, not by Troup himself, but by the spineless management who had sold him. They were concerned that the team lacked ambition, and that they were only out for lining their own pocket – a charge that has been made against Dundee directors all through the twentieth century.

In truth, it cannot be denied that Dundee's consistent underachievement throughout the twentieth century can be traced to the sometimes unnecessary sale of star players. The departure of Ure, Gilzean and Cooke in the 1960s would similarly lead to a long barren spell and a rather too close encounter with bankruptcy and extinction. Yet it is hard to be too critical of Dundee FC at this point. Dundee was a rich enough city, but not enough of the wealth was in the hands of those who supported Dundee FC, namely the workers in the jute mills. The workers were traditionally and notoriously ill-organised, with the result that they were badly paid. The visit of Hearts could attract a gate of only 12,000 – which was not really enough. There was also the undeniable fact that the deluxe North Stand had yet to be paid for.

Dundee's supporters, of course, forgave their team – eventually. But the next home game was a Scottish Cup tie against Second Division St Bernards. Dundee should have hammered them. In fact, it was a 0-0 draw and boos and catcalls punctuated the air. The luckless Davie Halliday, normally well-liked by the Dens Park faithful, was the main target. He was played on the left wing, not his favourite place – and he as he would readily have admitted himself, he was no Eckie Troup. He was not the only man like a fish out of water that particular Saturday however. The Duke of York was prevailed upon to forsake his new fiancée for one Saturday and visit Hampden Park to see Queen's Park *v.* Bathgate. It was a 1-1 draw and one wonders what the aristocratic and sheltered Duke made of the deserted Hampden and the lashing rain.

On this day, Troup was playing for Everton against Stoke. It was a heavy defeat for the Toffees to the tune of 4-1, but the correspondent of the *Liverpool Echo* was impressed:

> There could be no doubting the class of Troup when he was on the move.
> He did not run along the wing and lift the ball into the centre heedless of
> his colleagues' positions, but he placed the ball well and also made use of
> a delicious inward pass, as deceptive as it was neatly done.

The Everton team that day was Harland: Raitt and Downs; Fleetwood, Hart and Grenyer; Chedgzoy, Peacock, Cock, Williams and Troup.

Following this game, Everton then had a week of enforced leisure while the Fourth Round of the FA Cup was being played, but then came an important couple of games against Chelsea. In these days, in the English League, games were played back to back home and away. Troup's home debut was thus on 10 February. The following Wednesday, both teams reappeared at Stamford Bridge. In his Goodison debut Troup impressed, as did right winger Chedgzoy and Everton won 3-1. The scores were reversed at Stamford Bridge, however.

There followed a couple of very impressive wins against Middlesbrough, but the good was undone by feckless displays against Oldham. Troup scored his first goal for Everton at Bolton on 30 March (Good Friday), and such was the enthusiasm of the supporters for the young Scotsman that there was now a buzz about the team that had been absent for some time.

It must have been difficult for the small town Scottish young man to adapt to the vastly different life of the Merseyside metropolis. Liverpool teemed with humanity in those days in the same way that Glasgow did. Appalling poverty co-existed with affluence, disabled ex-soldiers roamed the streets begging for financial help, the ladies of the night plied their trade near the docks. On one occasion, already referred to, in summer 1919 Liverpool had an industrial relations rarity – the police (the 'scrubbers' as they were less than affectionately called) went on strike, and law and order simply broke down. In addition, the proximity to Ireland (then in full civil war) meant another influx of Irish people trying to avoid the conflict. It also meant that there was a trade in arms.

*Alec with his wife, Elizabeth, shortly after their wedding in 1923.*

Troup must have had a problem with the Scouse accent, for his own broad Forfar Doric was almost far enough away to cross the border of 'mutual unintelligibility' which linguists tell us defines a language rather than a dialect. He may have been homesick, but this was not reflected in his play, which continued to raise eyebrows – and in any case he was about to do something about his homesickness.

Troup had left Forfar Station on Thursday 25 January. This was of course Burns day, a matter of more importance to Scots people in those days than it is now. The local press tells us that Eckie had a reputation as a tenor as well as a footballer, but laments sadly that any Burns songs that he would sing to Liverpudlians would be as 'pearls to swine'. Much mention is also made of the unfortunately-named Jack Cock, an England internationalist who was now with Everton. Everton would take 'some stopping' as Troup teamed up with him. Both were also entertainers, Troup as a singer and Cock as a music hall artiste, the latter not slow to exploit the earning possibilities of his name. Troup himself was quoted as saying that he is looking forward to meeting Jack, and also that he would not be completely lost at Everton, for his old friend Davie Raitt would be waiting for him at the station.

But he would not be the only Forfarian departing for Liverpool in early 1923. Some time later, in conditions of the greatest secrecy, Elizabeth Kidd followed the same route, and on Wednesday 4 April 1923 they were married at a Registry Office in Liverpool. There was no sinister reason for the secrecy, other than that the two of them had no desire for publicity. Alec being as always a profoundly shy individual, was also keen to protect Elizabeth from the glare of the press, whose intrusion was exhibited in another Forfarshire marriage that spring – that of the Duke of York and Elizabeth Bowes-Lyon, which was due to take place at the end of the month.

*The Courier,* however, claimed that their man got to know about it. 'Man, how did you get to know?' it claims that Troup said. This is unlikely. Troup would surely have said 'Foo did you get tae ken, min?' In any case, *The Courier* wished them all the best. Not that they needed it. It was a very happy marriage, with Alec devoted to his lovely Elizabeth. They came north to Forfar on honeymoon a few days later (perhaps to make their peace with any relatives who might have disapproved of the secrecy and the haste) and it was hard to imagine a happier couple. Their love and respect deepened over the years, Elizabeth even referring to him in the house by his football nickname of 'Troupie'!

The season ended with Everton fifth in the table – a great deal higher than they might have expected, and certainly higher than in 1922, when they were third from the bottom and lucky to escape relegation. But the Champions of 1923 were city rivals Liverpool (for the second year in a row), and even as far back as the 1920s, that hurt! They were thirteen points ahead of Everton and that was thirteen points too many. Everton had not won the Championship since the unreal circumstances of 1915.

But the Goodison fans had reason to believe that the tide was turning in their favour. Crowds had steadily gone up to see their new Scottish genius, and very soon they were saying in Merseyside what they had said on Tayside and in Forfar, namely that Alan Morton had to be some player if he could keep Troup out of the Scottish team. Indeed, on 14 April 1923, the very day that Scotland and England were drawing 2-2 at

Hampden Park, Troup had a brilliant game as Everton beat Aston Villa 2-1, scoring a goal in his 'inimitable style', running into the centre to hammer home a Parry through ball.

The last home game of the season was on 28 April, when a Cock goal was enough to beat Preston North End at Goodison. This piece of news was, however, dwarfed by the performance of another Lancashire team – Bolton Wanderers, who beat West Ham United 2-0 that day in the first ever Wembley Cup Final. The newspapers were full of stories of overcrowding and a policeman on a white horse who restored order – something that tended to overshadow Bolton's fine achievement.

But Everton supporters, with traditional jealousy of other local teams, were unimpressed by all this. They were more interested in the possibilities of what might happen with their own side now that they had the diminutive Scotsman on the left wing. He did indeed cut a funny figure on the wing with his lack of inches and self-effacing smile and gait, but the laughing would stop whenever the game began.

In fact, there was a new style and flair to the Everton team. Newspapers said things like 'Troup's dandy runs and dribbles have captivated the Mersey crowd', 'Troup has put the 'ton' back in Everton', 'Troup is bringing out the best in players like Cock and Chadwick' and 'Not since Tommy McDermott's dribbling runs have we seen such magic than in the charismatic little Scot'. The future looked very bright indeed for Troup and for Everton.

Not the least of Troup's problems would have been adapting to a new style of football. This is always the case, of course, when any footballer moves to another club, but in the 1920s there probably was a fundamental difference between Scottish and English football. Scottish football relied more upon the individual, the great, talented player who in one moment could turn a game. English football was faster with far more emphasis placed on speed and teamwork. This might at first sight have caused a few problems for Troup, who was certainly a talented individual, on whom Dundee had relied perhaps rather too much to produce the goods in the shape of the mazy run, the accurate cross and the drive for goal.

Yet if Troup learned anything from his First World War experiences, it was that the concept of the 'team' and the 'group' were important. It is always vital that team-mates should 'get on' in the social sense as well as the playing side. In this respect, Alec had few problems. His shy and retiring disposition did not hide any character weakness, and he was always able to mix socially and join in the general dressing room banter and conversation.

In Troup's case, it was only a small step from this to 'getting on' with his team-mates on the field. His first two or three games for Everton may have been difficult, but he very soon learned and became successful on two counts – one of fitting in to the general team plan, and also, more than occasionally, turning on his individual brilliance.

There was also the undeniable fact that football in England was bigger (although not necessarily better). The sheer size of the population would see to that, and in the city of Liverpool there was also the rivalry between Everton and Liverpool. Although this rivalry was (and remains) fundamentally friendly, unlike that in Glasgow for example, Troup was often taken aback by the intensity of the emotions. A feature, for example, of the 1920s was the introduction of a half-time scoreboard, on which the scores of

*Alec at training for Everton. Note the running spikes on his shoes. By all accounts, Alec was pretty swift over 100 yards.*

*Everton, 1923/24. From left to right, back row: W. Brown, Mr Barks (director), T. Fern, J. Elliott (trainer), D. Livingstone, F. Forbes, J. MacDonald, Mr Coffey (director), W. Chadwick. Front row: S. Chedgzoy, R. Irvine, J. Cock, H. Hart (captain), W. McBain, A. Troup.*

other games would be placed against a letter which appeared in a programme. Shortly after half time at Goodison Park, the results would be put up, and Troup would be amazed at the loud cheering which would break out when somebody was taking a very ordinary throw-in. This would be because the board said 'A 1-0', a coded message that, for example, Aston Villa were leading Liverpool by one goal to nil.

This city rivalry was something that Troup had never really encountered before, for Dundee's nearest rivals were Aberdeen. Dundee United (then called Dundee Hibs) were a poor Second Division outfit, who were looked upon patronisingly and conde-scendingly by Dundee supporters. Liverpool and Everton (and their supporters) on the other hand saw themselves as equals with now one team, now another holding sway. Thus, although Troup could walk through the streets of Dundee and if recognised, be greeted with cheers and good-natured well wishes, he soon realised that it was not always a good idea to travel on buses or trams in Liverpool late at night where he could often receive a totally different type of welcome.

Things like that prevented Troup from ever entirely losing his homesickness but, the season over, he could now enjoy a long summer holiday in 1923. While he was at Dundee, the wages were never entirely adequate to cover the 'close' season as well, but life was now a lot more prosperous for the Troups. They came north for a part of their holiday to their beloved Forfar and spent a day or two in Glen Clova, the loveliest of Angus's glens. But by late July, it was back to Liverpool and a fresh beginning for the start of season 1923/24. Training would begin on 1 August – and it would be intense.

Troup's first full season with Everton was a good one for himself, although the team in general would have been disappointed to finish seventh in the League. 'No team in the country has served up more delightful football than Everton,' said the *Liverpool Echo*, but there was as yet no tangible gain. This year's champions were Huddersfield Town, and Liverpool slipped badly. Everton had the satisfaction of beating Liverpool twice in the two back-to-back games in early October, but the team was generally mediocre and it was only a late season flourish in which they won their last four fixtures over the Easter weekend that kept them out of the bottom half of the table. A sub-standard performance on the south coast against Brighton and Hove Albion in early February saw another disappointing exit from the FA Cup, the trophy being won by Newcastle United.

Troup's form was good. He played in 41 of the 42 League games – only an ankle knock on 29 September keeping him out of the game against Huddersfield Town – but he only scored one goal, in a game against Aston Villa at Goodison on 12 September. This was because he was under orders to stay on his wing. He was not to wander inside as he had done at Dundee and Forfar (where of course he had been an inside left, in any case). His job was to reach the bye-line and cross for one or other of the three 'C's – Chedgzoy, Chadwick or Cock – to finish the job. The last named player, of course, continued to cause trouble for the headlines writers. In the absence of salacious tabloids who would nowadays enjoy themselves with all the puns and sexual innuendoes of the day, writers in the *Liverpool Echo* had to be much more circum- spect. His Christian name, Jack, would frequently be employed to spare the blushes of the genteel readers.

Troup did have his bad days of course – he would recall with embarrassment the 0-4 thrashing at Bramall Lane against Sheffield United – but there were other days when he was positively inspired. The Liverpool papers tried very hard to get him back into the Scotland team, but by his very nature of being an Anglo-Scot (i.e. a Scotsman who played for an English team), Troup was now at a disadvantage. In any case, it would have been extremely hard to prove a case against Alan Morton, whom the Scottish selectors saw regularly, and as Rangers won the league that year, no one could say that Alan's form was dipping. Alec, however disappointed he was, would shrug his shoulders and continue his job. A patriot too, he had two reasons to be happy about 12 April 1924. Everton had just beaten Tottenham 5-2 at White Hart Lane, and then about an hour later, as the Everton team were having their evening meal in a hotel before getting the train back up north, a Scotsman with a kilt and a tammy came up to Troup and told him that Scotland had drawn 1-1 in their first ever visit to Wembley.

Troup would have been impressed by the number of motor cars that were now around in Liverpool. He thought about getting one, but they were expensive and not always very reliable. Perhaps another new invention of the modern age would be a better idea – a radio or wireless as they were called. Elizabeth liked music, and there was lots of it on the radio. And at 6.15 p.m. on a Saturday, a man would read out all the football results – even the Scottish ones, so that he could know how Dundee and even Forfar Athletic had done!

There was another change in 1924 which he had never thought possible – Britain had a Labour Government. Alec was no politician – he would tend to vote Liberal because he had a vague belief that they stood more for fair play to everyone – but he had once heard, long before the war, in the I.L.P. Hall in East High Street, Forfar, a charismatic figure called Keir Hardie talking about a 'new Jerusalem' and a 'worker's paradise'. Now another Scotsman, Ramsay McDonald, was the first ever Labour Prime Minister – but there was sadly no sign of any great levelling out of wealth. McDonald's minority government would not see the year out, but it was at least a start.

For some reason or other, Elizabeth was never really happy in Liverpool. She and Alec stayed in digs with a Mr and Mrs Brown, but her heart was never there. In addition, Alec was all too aware that their stay in Liverpool might not be a permanent or even a lengthy one. All too often, he had seen how an injury or a loss of form had resulted in a sudden departure. For all these reasons, they decided against buying a house in Liverpool, but settled instead at Stark's Close, Forfar. Alec stayed with the Browns in Liverpool during the season, but came home as often as he could.

*Everton's squad for 1924/25. From left to right, back row: J. MacDonald, W.F. Rooney, J. Kendall, S. Chedgzoy, F.C. Stephenson, D. Bain, A.I. Harland, A.E. Virr. Second row: H. Makepeace, R. Irvine, G.R. Caddick, D. Livingstone, W. Brown, N. McBain, J. Kerr, E. Barton, E. Storey. Third row: T.H. McIntosh, J. Fare, D. Raitt, J. McGrae, J. Peacock, J.G. Cock, D. Reid, D. Kirkwood, J. Fortune, J. Smith. Fourth row: H. Cooke, H. Houghton, A. Wall, F. Parry, H. Hart, W. Chadwick, F.J. Forbes, F. Hargreaves, J. Elliott. Front row: W.D. Williams, A. Troup, C.E. Glover.*

This was not perhaps as unusual or crazy an idea as it might first appear. Travel by train was, if anything, better in the 1920s than it is now, with an easy connection to Forfar Station. This rail connection ran until it was closed down in 1967. Although a six-hour train journey was not pleasant, Troup's wages were such that the fares were easily coped with, and Alec would be happy sitting anonymously in a corner reading a newspaper or a book, often listening with amusement to supporters discussing football in a loud voice and occasionally even mentioning his name, without realising who he was!

One particular occasion, he recalled with a chuckle. As the train pulled out of Glasgow one night, with Troup sitting in the corner of a compartment, a few Rangers supporters came in. They had had a drink or two, but were not offensive. They talked in raucous voices about the 'wee society man', as they called Alan Morton, and said that he was the greatest. They (naturally) ridiculed the international pretensions of Celtic's Adam McLean, but one of them admitted that he had seen Troup when he was with Dundee and had been very impressed with him. One of them offered Alec a drink at this point, which Alec politely refused, and asked him 'What dae you think, mac?' Alec smiled and quietly agreed that Alan Morton was indeed a great player. The Rangers supporters were apparently unaware to whom they were talking.

At the end of the 1923/24 season, Everton went on tour to Catalonia, in north-east Spain, to play 'the Barcelona Football Club'. It would be a short tour, and neither the *Liverpool Echo* nor anyone else seems to have thought it worth reporting. Details, however, are found in Thomas Keates' *History of the Everton Football Club*. They are sparse and patronising, giving the impression that Everton were doing the Spaniards a great favour in visiting them. But, he said, 'the teams of the Barcelona Club played a surprisingly good game', for Everton won the first game 2-1 and lost the second 1-2. The highlight of the tour, however, came when Everton faced Newcastle United (the season's FA Cup winners, complete with mighty men like Hudspeth and Seymour) and beat them 3-2 on 21 May. This was to give the Spaniards the opportunity of watching 'two John Bulls fight in their arenas against each other'. What they made of the diminutive, fair-haired Scotsman on the wing is not recorded.

These tours by British teams to all parts of Europe were fairly common in the 1920s. Everton, mercifully, did not suffer the same fate as Raith Rovers did a season earlier when, en route to the Canary Islands, they were shipwrecked off the coast of Galicia in north eastern Spain! The tours were not taken too seriously and were a great opportunity for players to see a bit of the world, have a holiday and allow the clubs to earn money by drawing big gates to see a British team take on some undemanding local opposition.

1924/25 was a less happy year for both Troup and Everton. The team finished 17th in the First Division, something which their huge support considered unacceptable, even though Thomas Keates in his *History of Everton* quotes the lisping Lord Dundreary who stated that 'thith ith one of thothe thingth a fella can't underthtand'. Troup sustained a bad knee injury in December and missed a total of ten League games as well the FA Cup games. Everton actually reached the fifth round that year before going out to Sheffield United, the eventual winners. Without a shadow of a doubt, Troup's absence was critical.

Troup's return in March saw an improvement in the team's form and a few wins which were necessary to stave off relegation, but the significant event that year (for both Everton and Troup) was the signing of a seventeen-year-old boy from Tranmere Rovers, just across the Mersey, in March. The *Liverpool Echo* had been singing the praises of this lad for some time, and Everton fans were looking for him to score the goals which had been so lacking since the injuries and loss of form of Jack Cock. The boy's name was William Ralph Dean, and even before he came to Everton, his curly hair and somewhat swarthy complexion had given him the nickname 'Dixie'. It would be some time however before this transfer would pay dividends.

On Easter Saturday, 11 April 1925, Everton beat Blackburn Rovers 1-0, a goal from Troup's left-wing partner Fred Kennedy (who had recently joined them from Manchester United for £2,000), more or less dispelling any lingering fear of relegation. But Troup might have been forgiven if his mind had been less than totally on the game. His thoughts may well have drifted back to Scotland, to Hampden Park in Glasgow, where his old mates of Dundee were playing in the Scottish Cup final. Their opponents were Celtic, who were no great shakes these days and certainly not a patch on their fine pre-war side.

Troup had given an interview for the *Dundee Courier* a few days before the Scottish Cup final, and had wished Dundee well, saying that he thought they could do it. There may even have been a touch of homesickness and nostalgia in what he said, and he certainly must have wondered if he had done the right thing in coming to Everton. He could have been having a real taste of the big time in Scotland, whereas his move to Everton had brought him more money and a higher standard of football, but as yet no great success – and no glamorous games like a Cup final.

Troup had arranged for the reporter of the *Liverpool Echo* to tell him the half-time and the full-time score from Hampden. The press box now had telephone and telegraph facilities, and news could travel fast. At half time, as he came off the park, the reporter told him that Dundee were winning 1-0, and that someone called McLean had scored. Davie McLean! Troup's old Forfar pal was still playing for Dundee, in a professional career which had begun in 1907 and still had a long way to go.

Troup was thinking he could have a look at Davie's medal in the summer – in fact he wouldn't have to ask, for Davie would be brandishing it about anyway– but would Celtic fight back? In fact they did, and Troup finished the game for Everton knowing nothing about Patsy Gallacher's wonder equalizer, nor Jimmy McGrory's late winner. All the reporter could say was that Celtic had won 2-1. If Troup had stayed with Dundee, would he have won that Cup for them?

But business interests now became very important for Alec. He was aware that he was now thirty, and that, although he was fit and trained hard, his football career would not last for ever. He decided to do something that he had been mulling over in his mind for some time. He was always himself a very neat dresser, looking very dapper and well turned out. Why didn't he invest some of the money that he had earned (particularly from his transfer fee to Everton) in a draper's business? With his wife now domiciled

*GET YOUR CAP*

. . AT . .

# A. TROUP'S.

## MEN'S and BOYS' UNDERWEAR.

*Nice Selection in*

TIES, SOCKS, HANDKERCHIEFS, &c.

RADIAC SHIRTS

*To suit all tastes and at Keenest Prices.*

# A. TROUP,

## *CORNER HAT & CAP SHOP,*

### 26 Castle Street, Forfar.

# George Langlands,

## Joiner,

## 29 EAST HIGH STREET, FORFAR.

Estimates given for all kinds of Joiner Work.

*An advertisement for Alec's shop, from the Forfar Directory of 1927.*

in Forfar, she or some other relative could run the business while he was still playing football. In fact, as long as he was playing, it would be good advertising for the business. It was a gamble, but he decided to buy a shop in Castle Street at the junction with Queen Street. That it would turn out to be a good investment would be proved in future years. But he still had a few years football left in him.

The season of 1925/26 was the first one in which the Troup-Dean combination began to work. Dean scored 32 goals, most of them coming from either of the two wingers. On the right was Sam Chedgzoy, a good ball player and ball winner, but also very fast and direct, whereas Troup on the left was more subtle, more creative. From both of them, Dean fed avidly. Troup himself played in every game bar four – due to injuries in December and a recurrence in January, and then for a far happier reason in April, namely that he was away playing for Scotland.

Yet the defence leaked goals, often losing them at vital points of the game – there is an astonishing statistic that 11 out of the 42 League games ended up as 1-1 draws! As a result of this, Everton finished 11th in the League, and there was the usual dismal performance in the third round of the FA Cup, not for the first time against a lower division side. This time it was Fulham who held Everton to a 1-1 draw at Goodison, and then scraped through 1-0 at Craven Cottage on the following Thursday.

There was one horrendous defensive display at Roker Park, Sunderland, on 10 October, where seven goals were given to an incredulous Sunderland side, and this while the combination of Troup and Dean scored three for Everton! Probably Troup's best day that season was on 24 April, the week after he had been in the successful Scotland team that had beaten England 1-0. On his return from international duty, on that particular day at Goodison, Alec was cheered on to the park (for many Evertonians will be very happy to desert England if one of their men is playing for the opposition) and then gave a quite delightful display of football as, almost on his own, he took Newcastle United apart and laid on three goals for Dean.

But Everton were still not winning any silverware. Huddersfield won the League again, and the Cup went to Bolton who beat Manchester City in the final. Next season would be different however. A change in the offside rule, to encourage more goals and kill the defensive offside trap of some teams, would make a big difference. Would it help Troup and Everton in their quest for more goals, however?

This was not, however, the immediate concern. Summer 1926 saw three things happen, none of them directly to do with football – but they all impinged on the life of Alec Troup. Just as the football season was ending, the General Strike occurred. To say that this was merely a dispute between the miners and the government of Baldwin and Churchill is of course facile, for it affected everyone. The final game of Everton's season was against Bolton Wanderers (a 2-0 win) on 1 May, and Troup had the wit to get on a train north as fast as he could before the strike started on 3 May.

In the event, the General Strike did not last two weeks, but at the time no one knew that and there was the feeling that it could have lasted for years. It was perceived as a threat to the democratic way of life, and fingers pointed to what had happened in Russia in 1917 or even in Italy in 1922, to suggest how it might all end. Words like 'insurrection' and 'civil war' were heard, even from people and politicians who really ought to have known better. Winston Churchill, for example, now firmly ensconced in the Conservative government, was quite happy to be quoted as wanting to 'starve the bastards out'.

Forfar had no great history or tradition of militancy, and support for the strike was lukewarm. But the town was besieged, as it were, by Fife miners who swaggered around the streets, trying to persuade people not to go to the factories and indulging in some threatening behaviour. In particular, an attempt was made to picket Forfar Station to prevent a delivery of bobbins (necessary for continuous jute production) to the factories. Had these bobbins remained in the station warehouse, the factories would have had to close.

The response of the gaffer (foreman) of the 'Mull' (a factory in South Street) was to send a horse and cart with a driver and a young apprentice to collect these bobbins. The driver of the cart was a man who had been injured in the face and mouth in the First World War, and consequently was afflicted with a speech impediment; however, even before the war, he had had a reputation of being the most surly, awkward, foul-mouthed and unco-operative man in town.

The result was that on Wednesday 5 May, the pickets were in place at the station when a horse and cart drove up. The conversation (as told in later years with great relish by the young apprentice) probably went along these lines:

'Whaur are ye gaun? Ye cannae go in here. This is a picket'
'I coudnae gie a muck aboot that. I'm here mur muckin dobbins'
'What?'
'Dobbins! Ae ye muckin deef, ye dozent tunt? I've goat a muckin joab tae dae. Get oot o my muckin road!'

The miners stared at each other in puzzlement, and old Wull, realising that his star was in the ascendancy, continued in rich vein about Loos, Ypres, war dodgers, conscientious objectors and 'you tunts never muckin sa' an angry Merman', finishing up with 'get oot o ma muckin road – I muckin bide here and I'm mucked if ah'm gaena muckin tak oarders aff o' tunts like you'.

The combination of the Forfar accent, the foul language and Wull's deliberate saying of things that they would not understand was too much for the not particularly bright miners. In addition, a man with an obvious facial disfigurement like that – a war wound – earned a certain respect and the word 'Dobbins' (which they picked up in Wull's vitriolic, venomous and foul-mouthed diatribe) might have been something to do with food for his horse, which looked indeed as if its best days were behind it. The beast could not be allowed to starve! So they let him through.

Wull and the amazed young lad with him calmly drove into the station, loaded the cart with bobbins and came out again to a respectful wave from the pickets. To the horror of the young apprentice who had feared for his person, Wull became sociable and said that he liked watching East Fife and Raith Rovers when they came to Station Park, but that Morris and Collier of Raith Rovers were not nearly as good as Troup.

'Wee Eckie Troup, the best weenger in the hale of muckin Britain. He met the Keeng

*Everton, 1926/27. Alec is seated second from the right in the front row, and his friend, the great Dixie Dean, is third from left in the front row.*

ae day, and a-body said 'Fa's that wi Eckie Troup? Ha! Ha! Ha!' The horse and cart then disappeared down North Street to the 'Mull', with Wull telling the young apprentice that you didn't give in to 'tunts' like that. 'Sodgers! They never muckin' saw sodgers!' As a result of this combination of patriotism and sheer foul temper, the 'Mull' kept working all through the strike.

The General Strike did not last, of course. The TUC caved in and everything returned to a degree of normality by mid-May, although the embittered coalworkers continued their strike for some time. In early June, however, Troup received disturbing news. Dixie Dean, who had made such an impact with Everton, was involved in a motorcycle accident in Wales, and had suffered from severe head injuries.

Motorcycles were a common form of transport in the 1920s, particularly among football players. Footballers did not quite earn enough to buy a motor car in those days, but motorcycles (themselves a status symbol) were very common. Troup remembered, of course, that Sunny Jim Young of Celtic, who had fouled him so mercilessly that day in 1914, had met his death in a motor cycle accident in 1922.

This accident (from the sketchy details that reached Troup) sounded serious. It soon became apparent that Dean would survive, however, in spite of a very pessimistic prognosis at the outset, but the question remained as to whether he would ever play football again. This meant a great deal to Troup, for Dean was one of the few centre forwards with the ability to rise to Troup's crosses.

Troup went to the West Derby Nursing Home to see Dean in his recuperation and was soon reassured that he would play again and that his heading ability would not be impaired in spite of the plates that had been inserted in his head to repair his fractured skull. Dean was in good spirits and already looking forward to the start of the season, although he was aware that it would be a week or two before he was fit.

But another matter needed Alec's attention back in Forfar. At 8 Stark's Close, where they had been living for some time, his wife gave birth to a baby girl on Thursday 5 August in the early hours of the morning. Nan, as she was called, would be the only child that the Troups were to have, and naturally Alec and Elizabeth were delighted. Alec had been meant to report to Goodison for training a day or two earlier, but had of course been given special dispensation. Interestingly enough, the birth certificate (registered on 14 August) gives the father's occupation as a 'Gents Outfitter' rather than 'Professional Footballer' – a clear indication that for Alec, playing football was now a sideline to the necessity of having to provide a long-term solution to the problems of feeding a family.

He thus returned to Liverpool a few days after that for the new season. He was now a proud father, but without Dean, Everton would have a struggle this season. In fact, Troup, either because of a recurrence of the old shoulder injury or because Mr McIntosh felt that Troup would be better out of contention until Dean returned, did not play until 18 September and it is no accident that Everton had a shocking start to the season with five straight defeats. Dean eventually returned on 23 October.

Troup did, however, play in Everton's first win of the season – and a remarkable win it was too. It was the Merseyside derby against Liverpool on 25 September. Although all derbies are 'must win' situations, this one really was – otherwise sackings and resignations would surely follow. A total of 43,973 fans were at Goodison to see the game – a tense, closely-fought game won by a single goal scored by Troup's left-wing partner, O'Donnell. Troup had a splendid game, but he did not hang around for post-match celebrations.

He had an important date in Forfar the following day – Baby Nan's christening in the Church of Scotland. The Old Church (the 'Big Kirk' as the locals called it) was full on this occasion, and Reverend W.G. Donaldson would enjoy himself, as he always did with a large congregation. He was an interesting man– a fine Biblical scholar, a good orator (nicknamed 'Knockie' for his propensity to thump the pulpit table when upbraiding people for their sinfulness) and much-loved around the town, in spite of his somewhat ferocious countenance. He was of course 'the Minister' in the days when that meant a lot, and he was always treated with respect and admiration, not least for his assiduous attention to his parishioners in times of family crisis. In the summer of 1914, before the First World War broke out, he had been to the Holy Land on holiday. He had filled a canister full of water from the River Jordan (filthy, brackish stuff by all accounts) and brought it home. Thus for the next few years, Forfar infants were baptised with the water that Jesus himself had been baptised with!

Sadly, it had run out by 1926 and the Troups' baby had to make do with the local reservoir water. 'Knockie' preached well as always, and the local people had a chance to see their local hero. The ladies would of course drool over the baby, but the men stared at the unpretentious little man who was now unquestionably the greatest living Forfarian, who had now played five times for Scotland. 'Knockie', a football fan himself, shook Alec's hand, assured him that he followed his progress in the paper, and wished him well. 'Knockie' would continue his ministry until one evening service in 1937 when he insisted on continuing to preach with a heavy cold against medical advice, and collapsed and died in the pulpit.

But it was now back to Liverpool for Alec and an attempt to save Everton from relegation – for that was what the papers were saying even as early as September. The return of Dean did give the team some sort of a boost, with 3 wins out of four games, but the defence was poor. Twice, five goals were conceded that season, and on another occasion Leicester scored 6. On 5 March, Newcastle (admittedly with Hughie Gallacher in inspiring form and en route to a Championship) put 7 goals past them in a game in which Everton also scored 3! Eventually, Everton escaped relegation by four points, but they were indebted to a Troup-inspired 3-1 defeat of Birmingham City in the third from last game of the season.

The FA Cup continued to disappoint Evertonians. This time it was Hull City in the fourth round who put them out after two draws. Troup had played every game from September and there were days when he seemed to be the only form of inspiration that Everton had. Dean scored 21 goals, but often seemed to lack sharpness and, due to his road accident, confidence. But he was also now playing for England, scoring (presumably to Troup's disgust) the two goals which beat Scotland at Hampden Park on 2 April 1927.

But Dixie had a greater moment of triumph just round the corner ... and Alec would be very much involved in it.

# 7

# TROUPIE AND DIXIE
## THE ANNUS MIRABILIS, 1927/28

Everton were, and are, a team which expects to win things. They are a team with an immense support who crave success. Even their Latin motto 'nil satis nisi optimum' – 'Nothing but the best is good enough' – reflects their aspirations. The problem is that success does not come all that often, although, depending on the method one uses, a case could be made out for saying that statistically, since records began, Everton are the most successful English club in history. Supporters of Liverpool and Manchester United would of course disagree!

Yet for Evertonians, the 1920s were disappointing. The League Championship had been won in 1891 and 1915 and the FA Cup in 1906 – and that was too long ago for their vast legion of fans. The 1920s were as difficult economically for the city of Liverpool as they were for other parts of the United Kingdom, and the outlook was not good.

The fact that the last honour had been won in the somewhat unreal wartime circumstances of 1915 was a source of a great deal of pain for these most earnest of supporters. So many Evertonians were aware that their ten-year-old son, for example, had never seen them winning anything. Even more poignant was the recollection, in many cases, that their fathers had been alive in 1915, perhaps had even seen a few games at Goodison that year but had then said their fond farewell to die in some far corner of some foreign field that was certainly not England, no matter what any poet might say. Since then there had been precious little to cheer up Evertonians. However, they were about to have their pay-off.

The season of 1927/28 opened with a game against Sheffield United at Goodison. Sheffield United had won the FA Cup some two years previously and were highly regarded in these days, but Everton simply swept them aside with the men from the steel town having no answer to the wiles of Troup. Troup scored and was responsible for at least two of the other goals in the 4-0 romp. In another game in the early part of the season against Birmingham City, when Everton hit 5, Troup scored two – one of them with his head. The scribes marvelled that such a small man could rise to score such a goal, but Troup, like a great deal of small players (one thinks of Celtic's Jimmy Johnstone in the 1960s and 1970s) was remarkably agile.

It was not, however, Troup's ability to score goals that lit Everton up that autumn (although he did score Everton's only goal in the 1-1 encounter with Liverpool) – it was has almost telepathic understanding with William Ralph Dean. Dean would be dubbed 'Dixie' by the fans – a nickname that he himself did not like, apparently, and one that owed its origins in those less politically correct times to what would now be described as racism. Dean had a dusky complexion and black curly hair, and as American slave songs were popular in the music hall, the name Dixie seemed appropriate. 'Is it true what they say about Dixie? Does the sun really shine on him?' was a song which was popular with the Everton fans, but it was certainly a very touchy subject as far as the otherwise genial and affable Dean was concerned.

It is perhaps wise at this point to differentiate between William Ralph 'Dixie' Dean of Everton and England in the 1920s and 1930s on the one hand and John 'Dixie' Deans of Celtic and Scotland in the 1970s on the other. Both were fine players, prolific goal-scorers and personality players in their respective eras and it is unfortunate that the similarity in their names will lead many people to confuse them. It is, of course, William Ralph Dean that we are here discussing. The other 'Dixie' owed his nickname, presumably, to the similarity of their surnames.

The chivalrous Dean would say many times afterwards that he owed so many of his goals to his friend Alec Troup, and a typical Dean goal would start with a pass from midfield finding the mercurial little winger. Dean would then charge up the middle at a parallel rate of knots to Troup. Troup had the ability to delay or to speed up accordingly, and the object of the exercise was to ensure that Dean was in the box in a goalscoring position before the opposing centre half was.

If this objective was achieved, Troup would then float over one of his hanging crosses which looked as if it were drawn onto Dean's forehead as if by magic, Dean would then pick his spot, and seconds later the net would bulge. Dean would then sometimes rush across to thank Eckie, other times the pair would wave to each other as Troup trotted back to the halfway line with a quiet, contented smile on his face.

Dean (and the rest of the Everton dressing room) continued to have difficulty in understanding what Troup said. Like many a Scotsman, the Scottish accent lingered with him and as Forfar has a particularly strong, distinctive 'broad' accent, communication was not always perfect. Troup had to take quite an amount of gentle mockery as Dean would often shout things like 'That's hutt, min' or 'Slide it ower noo, min' on the training ground.

Alec was not fazed by this however. Both he and rest of Everton knew that he was far too good a player for the mockery ever to be unkind. Even when Alec's size became a topic of conversation and questions were asked about whether Forfar should be called Toytown or the land of the pixies and the elves, Alec gave as good as he got without ever losing his temper. In fact, he would make jokes himself about Forfar – they would throw a tarpaulin over the steeple when the rain came on or unfold it and put it inside the Old Kirk; a Forfar man went to Liverpool and was amazed to discover that the general post office did not sell ham because in Forfar, the Post Office did indeed sell ham; a Forfar lady could not go on the Liverpool Underground because a notice said 'Dogs must be carried on escalators' – and she did not have a dog with her!

By the turn of the year, the Troup-Dean combination was so successful that the Toffees were quite clearly ahead of their rivals – the previous year's Champions Newcastle United (Hughie Gallacher and all), Cup winners Cardiff City and the perpetual challengers of the 1920s, Huddersfield Town. On Christmas Eve, Everton went to Arsenal and lost 3-2 (in spite of a fine goal by Troup), but recovered well to beat Cardiff on Boxing Day by 2-1 at Goodison. As was the custom in those days, both teams then faced each other on the next day at Ninian Park, and this time Cardiff won.

The year of 1927 closed with Everton's fourth game in a week, and this time they won by beating Sheffield Wednesday 2-1 at Hillsborough. Although Everton had dropped points over the Christmas period, so did everyone else and they were still quite clearly top of the League and not showing any great sign of a permanent loss of form. With Dean still flourishing from Troup's crosses, the future looked bright.

That particular New Year's Eve, Troup may well have experienced feelings of mostalgia and homesickness, as Scotsmen often do in England. He may well have thought of the crowds at The Cross in his native Forfar, watching the clock on the steeple creep round to 12 o'clock, the hugging, kissing, well-wishing and, of course, the drink, consumed in excessive quantities by people anxious to forget the grim reality of life in those appalling jute mills. In Alec's case there were thoughts for his wife and small daughter too. But, for Alec, there was professional football, and another game to be played on 2 January.

He did indeed have much to console himself with. The team was playing well and he personally had every reason to be happy about his performances – the only blot on the horizon being his apparent inability to win back his place in the Scottish international team. This bothered Alec for he was very patriotically Scottish – although he had to admit that Alan Morton, 'The Wee Blue De'il', was very good. On his day, though, Troup felt that he could do better. On one point, however, Eckie was adamant. He could not go along with the belief that Morton was in the Scottish team only because there was a large Rangers support to appease. Alan was a fine player, and Alec remained on friendly terms with the gentlemanly, middle-class and refined man.

Dean was now in the throes of overtaking all previous Everton records for goals-coring, but 1928 got off to a mixed start. On Monday 2 January, in a derby at Ewood Park, Blackburn, defensive frailties saw Everton go down 2-4. However, Everton rectified matters on the following Saturday when they beat Middlesbrough 3-1 in a game which saw Dean break the Everton goalscoring record. It was not the only record that he was destined to break that year, of course, and it was significant that in the midst of all the back-slapping and congratulations on the field, the player that Dixie himself put his arms round was the diminutive Scotsman, Alec Troup.

But the customary early exit from the FA Cup, this time at the hands of Arsenal in Highbury in late January, seemed to put a dampener on Everton's League challenge as well, and very soon they were beginning to lose ground to Huddersfield Town. Indeed, the week after the Cup defeat, Everton went to Huddersfield and lost heavily with, for once, Troup not being the best winger on the field. That honour belonged to Alec Jackson, another Scotsman, once of Aberdeen, who was soon to become one of the Wembley Wizards.

1928 was the year when those eleven amazing Scotsmen trounced England 5-1 – the most illustrious moment in Scottish football history until Celtic won the European Cup in 1967. Troup did entertain a few hopes that he might win back the outside left berth, but the nod went yet again to Alan Morton. Another Evertonian, Dixie Dean, would play in that match – for England.

Everton's poor run of form in the early spring of 1928, which imperilled their Championship challenge, can possibly be put down to three factors. One was the continuing defensive mistakes and the other two involved and affected Dixie Dean. Dixie was clearly influenced by the Wembley Wizards game of 31 March 1928, both in his determination to be picked for this most important of games and also, in retrospect, after the mauling he received at the hands of the expert Scottish defence. As Dixie would himself later admit, he hardly got a kick of the ball. It would have been better for Dean not to have been picked, but his absence from Everton scarcely mattered that day, as Troup inspired the Toffees to a 2-0 win at Roker Park, Sunderland.

But there was another factor at work that year, playing on the mental insecurity of the young Dean. Newspapers were not slow to notice that the existing record for goals scored in a season was 59 (by George Camsell of Middlesbrough during the previous season of 1926/27) and that Dixie would be on course to beat this. Such hype puts pressure on players. For all his glamour and superstar status, Dixie was a sensitive soul and felt himself under a great deal of stress.

Yet the Everton fans were not slow to give him every encouragement. Latching on to the Victorian music hall song 'Nellie Dean', the ever resourceful Toffees sang

> That's another goal you've scored, Dixie Dean,
> Another goal for our team, Dixie Dean,
> For when Troupie sends it o'er
> Above them all you'll soar,
> It'a goal, we love you, Dixie Dean!

Dixie would often confide in his great friend Alec Troup. Alec was not above a little mischief-making 'It's a guid thing I wisnae playin at Wembley – it wid hae been six', as any Scotsman is likely to say whenever Scotland beats England, but he also appreciated the pressure that his friend was under. He reassured him that the supply of crosses would keep coming and that all would be well. Dean would look across the table with affectionate sincerity at the unpretentious, earnest little Forfar man – a hero like himself, but a man whom you would pass in the street without another glance.

In that vital week between the Wembley game and the Easter weekend, Dean's confidence returned. Good Friday (6 April) attracted 60,000 to Goodison to see Blackburn Rovers. Dean scored twice, one of them a cut-back from Troup, as Everton won 4-1. The following day, they earned a draw at Bury, their only goal coming once again from the Troup-Dean combination. The draw was perhaps a slight blow but any feelings of disappointment were eased by the news that neighbours Liverpool had done them a good turn by defeating Huddersfield Town. Everton were now back at the top of the League, albeit only on goal average and Huddersfield had games in hand.

Manager Tom McIntosh stressed, however, that if Everton won their five remaining games, the pressure would tell on Huddersfield. Huddersfield had other commitments – they were also in the FA Cup final. On 14 April, Everton had a hard-earned win

*Everton – Champions, 1928. From left to right, back row: McIntosh (manager), Kelly, Hart, Davies, O'Donnell, Virr, Cooke. Front row: Critchley, Martin, Dean, Cresswell, Weldon, Troup.*

in a tussle at Bramall Lane, Sheffield 3-1, then the following Wednesday beat a tired Newcastle side 3-0 at Goodison. Then, on Saturday 21 April, they beat Aston Villa 4-2. This was Championship form from a team who had come on to their game at exactly the right time – and Dean was finding the net. Not only that, but with the introduction of George Martin to the inside right position, the whole forward line of Critchley, Martin, Dean, Weldon and Troup now functioned as a fast-flowing cohesive unit, a feature of their play being their ability to send cross balls to each other in the middle of the field – and at speed – as they all charged forward. Just as the opposition defence was beginning to concentrate its resources on Everton's left, Alec Troup could send a ball across the park to find Ted Critchley and catch the defenders flat-footed.

Rivals Huddersfield lost the FA Cup final at Wembley that particular day (21 April) to Blackburn Rovers, but still had more games to play than Everton. Dean's goal tally was now 53 and with only two games left to play, he required six to equal and seven to beat the record. Excitement rose at Goodison with two questions on everyone's lips. 'Would Everton win the Championship?' and 'Would Dixie take the record?'

Indeed, it would be hard to work out from the Liverpool newspapers which issue was the more important. Everton had not won the League in the twentieth century (if we discount the unreal success of 1915 when the country was at war) and it clearly meant a lot to their supporters. The newspapers made much of what had happened in Scotland to give a subliminal boost to Everton supporters. It is often thought that Everton supporters sympathise with Rangers, although attempts to label them the

'Orange' team of the city are clearly facile. But a couple of weeks previously, Rangers had broken their twenty-five-year hoodoo in the Scottish Cup when a famous Davie Meiklejohn penalty had set them on the way to a 4-0 win over rivals Celtic. Rangers, it was pointed out, had broken their jinx. Could Everton do the same?

On the other hand, Dixie's personal issue was massively important. A personality cult had grown up around this man in a way which it is difficult to parallel in other football clubs. Perhaps the closest analogy would be Geoff Boycott, the Yorkshire cricketer of the 1970s and 1980s. One often got the impression that neither Boycott himself, nor his many rabid supporters, were really too bothered about whether Yorkshire did well, for the main issue at stake was how well Boycott himself played.

Dean was not selfish however. He was a keen team man, and as desperate to win the Championship for the Everton fans as for any personal ambition. Yet, the thought of setting a record that would probably stand for all time (it is still standing in 2002) must have been a huge attraction. Fortunately, the interests did not really clash. Both things would happen if Dean kept on scoring goals.

On 28 April at Turf Moor, Burnley, Dean scored four as Everton won an exciting match 5-3. He injured himself, however, and doubts were now cast on his ability to recover, win the Championship for Everton and grab the record for himself.

In the event, the Championship was won anyway, for Huddersfield's League form

*Dixie's sixtieth goal of the 1927/28 season, scored at Goodison Park on 5 May 1928. Alec Troup (out of picture) had taken the corner, enabling Dean to soar above the defence and score.*

collapsed and even before the last game against Arsenal on 5 May, Everton had won the Championship. Huddersfield blew it in the last week, although they had a reasonable case to complain about fixture congestion. On the Monday night, they went down 1-0 to Sheffield United at home – something which gave Everton the initiative – and then at Villa Park, Birmingham, the Everton players (who had been taken to the game by their manager and directors) saw Villa win 3-0 – and the Championship was Everton's!

It is always strange to win a Championship without actually playing on the night that the victory was confirmed, but the feelings of elation were no less for all that. It had been a long struggle, as any League Championship always is, and it had been a long wait since 1915 or 1891, depending on how much credence one places on the wartime League victory. Nowadays, of course, one gets the impression that in some players' minds, the domestic Championship is merely a stepping stone on the way to European glory and more money, but in 1928, being Champions was a great achievement.

Back home in Dundee and Forfar, the news was greeted with a cocktail of delight and pride. The local press said things like 'Troup wins English League Championship,' as if the other Evertonians did not matter. This headline was on a par with the apocryphal but totally believable tale of how the sinking of the *Titanic* in 1912 was reported, namely 'Forfar Man Believed Drowned in Atlantic'! But Alec's wife and family were all delighted for him – and looked forward to seeing the medal. Alec was in fact the only 'ever-present' player in the Everton team of that year – and his contribution had been immense. In many ways, it was indeed Troup's Championship.

In Liverpool, Evertonians rejoiced. It was only their third Championship – the previous one being in wartime and the one before that, when Queen Victoria was still alive and well. The game on Saturday against the wealthy but under-performing Arsenal would now be the icing on the cake. Supporters could relax in the knowledge that the Championship was won – but there remained the other and scarcely less important matter of whether Dixie Dean could notch the record.

The League trophy, splendid with its blue ribbons, was on show at Goodison Park that early May Saturday, and even a microphone (about which some people were still suspicious) was installed so that everyone could hear the speeches at the end. But the speeches were not the main issue at stake. All eyes focussed on Dixie Dean. A hat-trick would clinch the record. He was fit. He scored one goal for Everton – a brilliant individual effort, then took a penalty-kick to equal the record. Then with time running out and the score at 2-2, Everton were awarded a corner on the left. Dean looked at his friend Eckie Troup as the wee man trotted over to take the corner. Dean glanced momentarily upwards. Troup knew what this meant – Dean wanted a high one.

Troup's determination equalled that of Dean himself. His ever-alert football mind went back to his days with Forfar North End at the Market Muir before the First World War. There he was always told about corners, 'If ye're gaeing tae float it in, min, hit it higher than ye think ye need. The wind'll get a haud o' it, and yer man'll be better able tae judge it. He'll hae time tae get in alo' it'. This is exactly what he did. As 60,000 held their breath, the ball floated in, high above the Arsenal defence until the curly-headed figure rose like a bird to connect and head the ball downwards past goalkeeper Paterson.

Goodison erupted as Dixie picked himself up, and ran to meet the ecstatic little Forfar man who was doing his own hops and skips to celebrate the success of his friend. Merseyside would talk about little else all summer. The record had been set – and remains till this day. And the record stays perhaps because there is no Alec Troup to make the goals for Alan Shearer or David Beckham!

We have an excellent account of this occasion in Thomas Keates' *History of The Everton Football Club 1878-1928*. Mr Keates was seventy-eight when he wrote this, and sadly never lived to see his book published. It is an excellent example of football prose written by a man who saw the founding of his beloved Everton fifty years earlier, and who, in 1928, clearly saw this moment as the greatest event in their history.

> We came to see the serious-dramatic, and find ourselves witnessing a serio-comic scenario. Five minutes from time we made up our minds that 'Dixie' wasn't going to get another goal, and that we were not going to win the match. Good heavens! While the thought was formulating, Troup (the electric tripper) [sic] sent a nice dropping shot in front of goal, the ball hung in the air, Dixie's magical head went for it, and tipped it into the net. You talk about explosions and loud applause; we have heard many explosions, and much applause in our long pilgrimage, but, believe us, we have never heard such a prolonged roar of thundering, congratulatory applause before as that which ascended to heaven when Dixie broke the record.
>
> The applause had some time to indulge itself while the ball made its way to the halfway line, to which the referee had pointed. The Arsenal goal-keeper could have kicked the ball as it lay crouching in the nest, but with feet of lead he approached it, mechanically picked it up with his hands, carried it out of the net, and then languidly kicked it down the field.

Meanwhile, a very comic episode intervened. 'Dixie' and the players had trooped to the half-way line, accompanied by deafening shouts of 'Good Old Dixie' and 'Well Done Dixie' etc.

> While 'Dixie' was bowing his head modestly in acknowledgement of the idolatrous storm, a low-comedy looking chap evaded the police and stumbling up to 'Dixie', managed to shake his hand. The game had to be suspended until he had been helped off the ground by a policeman.
>
> The first comedian's turn had been such a success, that a second was seen frantically rushing for 'Dixie's' hand; he got a shake, and before 'Dixie' realised it, the second comedian had kissed him. The patience of the referee was exhausted; he seized the second comedian by the scruff

of the neck and bundled him off the ground. While the unrehearsed comedy was being enacted, screams of laughter mingled with the storm of applause.

It really was about the most side-splitting, screamingly funny farcial [sic] comedy and extra turn that was introduced into a football match. There was no mistake about the spectators having enjoyed the inter-polation. 'Wouldn't have missed it for anything,' Dick, Tom and Harry declared.

When order was restored and the 'low-comedy looking chaps' were evicted, Arsenal actually equalized, but it made no difference – the day belonged to Everton. The League Championship trophy was duly presented to Everton's captain Warney Cresswell. It was without doubt the highlight of Alec Troup's career, marginally ahead, he always said, of the Scotland appearances which he always cherished dearly.

Troup himself scored ten goals that season, which is no bad haul for a winger, especially as he had also contributed to a large percentage of the centre forward's 60! He had also been lucky to have had a fine inside left partner in Tony Weldon, who had joined Everton from Airdrie and whom Troup felt to be unlucky not to be considered for international honours. The newspapers would often call him 'Well done, Weldon'. Another forager for Dean had been right-winger Ted Critchley, but Dean would always say that, with all due respect to the right wing, it was the left wing which produced the goods.

That night, the directors of the club broke with social convention by inviting the players to dine with them at the North Western Hotel, Liverpool. In the 1920s, the feudal system of separation of directors and players was seldom breached – but this was a special occasion. 'The bonhomie and camaraderie temperament of the Chairman', as Keates somewhat eccentrically puts it, 'infected the whole company and permeated the exultant speeches'. Dean spoke and singled out 'Alec'. No one seems to have disputed this assertion that it was Troup who had made Dean.

After this, it was the Empire Theatre on Monday for a spot of culture, some Shakespeare on Tuesday and a holiday tour to Switzerland on the Wednesday. This trip lasted a fortnight from 9 May to 23 May. Four games were played against Basle, Berne, Zurich and Geneva and all four were won in stifling heat in the somewhat primitive conditions of Swiss stadia. Basle were beaten 2-0, then Berne 5-0. Zurich then put up a better fight to lose 1-0, and the tour finished with a tight 3-2 win over Geneva in a close game. It was a tremendous experience for the Swiss, who flocked in droves to see the great Dixie Dean and the triumphant Everton team. No doubt Alec brought home clocks, watches and statuettes of William Tell for his wife and daughter, the latter now approaching her second birthday.

There was more joy for Alec when he won the Charity Shield – the annual trophy played for by the winners of the English League and the FA Cup. The Cup winners had been Blackburn Rovers, and thus it was an all-Lancashire tussle, played at Old Trafford on Wednesday 24 October 1928. Everton won 2-1, and it was the unbeatable combination of Troup and Dean once again. A few minutes before half-time, Troup ran down his

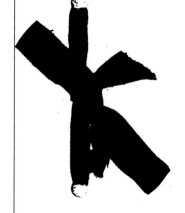

# The
# EVERTON
# FOOTBALL
# CLUB

# DINNER

*To Celebrate*

THE
## JUBILEE
OF THE CLUB,
1879 - 1929

—•—

PHILHARMONIC HALL,
LIVERPOOL,
*April 24th 1929.*

*The programme from Everton's jubilee dinner in 1929. Some historians claim that it was 1878 that Everton were founded, and that the jubilee dinner should have been celebrated in 1928. But, as Everton won the League in 1928, perhaps there were enough celebrations anyway.*

left wing and centred accurately for Dean to head home. It was the archetypal Troup/ Dean goal once again.

Blackburn fought back and levelled through Thornewell in the sixtieth minute. Extra time looked a certainty until Troup slipped a perfect ball through to Dean – on the ground this time rather than in the air – and Dixie finished clinically. Incredibly, Dean had been on international duty only forty-eight hours earlier, scoring the winning goal for England against Ireland at Goodison. Now in the Charity Shield, he and Troup won another medal. Sadly, there would be no more for Alec.

The Charity Shield is now the high profile pipe-opener to the English season. Usually it is played at Wembley. It is a shame that these circumstances did not prevail in 1928, for it would have given Alec the opportunity to play at the beautiful new stadium. Sadly, a combination of Alan Morton and Everton's repeatedly poor performances in the FA Cup prevented him from having the opportunity to grace the Wembley turf.

The Charity Shield was the apogee of Everton, but hereafter League form took a severe dip. Everton ended up 18th in 1928/29 and although they were never really likely to be relegated as Bury and Cardiff were so far below everyone else, they did distress their supporters by losing their last 6 games. One of these games, admittedly on a wet Tuesday in April, attracted a crowd of only 7,996 to Goodison, by some distance their poorest home crowd since well before the war.

The reasons for this slump in form were twofold. One was that the defence were simply not up to scratch, with goals being conceded at an alarming rate. They were particularly generous to Manchester City, who took six off them at Goodison in September and five at Maine Road in January. The other reason was that in the forward line, Dixie Dean was frequently injured, particularly in the latter half of the season, something that was quite likely to happen, given his bustling, physical style of play. With all due respect to Attwood and White who played in the centre forward position, they lacked the telepathic understanding which Dean and Troup shared, and although the crosses kept coming in, the golden head was not there waiting for them.

For Troup himself, the season had been a reasonably good one. He was out for four games around New Year with a recurrence of the shoulder injury. Troup's absence was possibly a major factor in Everton's pitiful display in the FA Cup, when they went out in the third round to Chelsea, thus continuing their dismal tradition in that tournament. By the end of the season, however, he had been made captain of the team, a tremendous tribute to his effort and endeavour. Yet, he must have been disappointed after the glories of the previous season. He was very aware that at the end of the season he would be thirty-four, and that his ambitions of playing in a major Cup final, either in England or Scotland, were beginning (like his hair) to recede.

The 1929/30 season saw Alec in the wilderness. An ankle injury in pre-season training meant that he lost his place to fellow Scot Jimmy Stein. Alec, being nominal captain of the side, had to be at every game to give moral support to the manager and to encourage the players. This he did, giving everyone the benefit of his experience and know-how, but he did not play until early December, when he scored in a 3-0 defeat of Grimsby. A creditable 0-0 draw with Manchester United followed, but then a defeat by Sheffield United and a return of the ankle injury on 21 December at Bramall Lane saw him miss the two Christmas games against Sheffield Wednesday, both heavy defeats. A panicky management now brought back the half-fit Troup for the game at Bolton on 28 December, and the team were soundly beaten, Troup made no impact and Everton were now deservedly anchored at the bottom of the League.

Troup was one of the scapegoats for this shocker, and in fact he never played again for Everton. Without him, the team continued to struggle and it was an indication of just how much they had owed to Alec when he was playing well. Alec, dropped and unhappy, was silently critical of the many managerial follies that were being perpetrated, but was far too much of a professional and a loyal friend to voice them. It is a lonely business when one is out of favour (especially when being in the embarrassing position of captain), and waves of homesickness were taking over in these early days of 1930. He had already decided that he was going home at the end of the season to concentrate on his business interests, and perhaps turning out on a part-time or amateur basis for his beloved Forfar Athletic. And then one day in late February, Mr McIntosh asked him into his office and told him that another club was interested in him.

Alec had heard a story that Rochdale might make a bid for his services, but his heart leaped when Mr McIntosh told him who the interested party was. It was Dundee!

# 8

# RETURN OF A HERO

## 1930-33

Back in Dundee, things had not been so good. Since Troup's departure in 1923, Dundee had suffered. There had been one appearance in the Scottish Cup Final in 1925 where, but for a superhuman performance by Celtic's Patsy Gallacher, the Cup would surely have been theirs. 1927 had seen a creditable fifth position in the League. But apart from that, the general pattern had been one of decline. In 1929, the team had finished up third bottom, and April had been an edgy month, with Dundee grinding out draws to retain their First Division status.

Now in the early months of 1930, the position, if anything looked even more precarious. In Dundee, as elsewhere, the icy blast of the recession was making its presence felt. One or two jute factories were closing down, and many more were on short-time working – just three days a week. In such circumstances, it was hardly surprising that match attendance was dropping, with quite a few home games failing to reach the five figure mark.

Manager Jimmy Bissett was an honest trier, but he lacked the charisma necessary for the job. In February 1930, something dreadful happened, further increasing the gloom which hung over Dens Park. It concerned Hughie Ferguson, the famous Scotsman who had taken the English Cup to Wales (he scored the only goal in the FA Cup final of 1927 when Cardiff City beat Arsenal). Now, his best days having passed, Hughie had been bought on the cheap by Dundee to offset the loss of some star players.

Sadly, Hughie, who had been an outstanding success for Motherwell in the early 1920s and was considered unlucky not to have earned a Scotland cap, was struggling. He was visibly slowing down and rumoured to be fond of a dram. He had been out of the team for some time when he told his landlady that he was off to see a 'talkie' picture at the cinema. The good lady had been worried about him because he was quite depressed sometimes, but he seemed fine that night. Hughie went up to Dens Park instead of the cinema and opened the gas tap in an enclosed room. It was clearly premeditated, with no suspicious circumstances according to the police.

Such things would make life even more difficult for any team, and form plummeted further. A defeat at the hands of Queen's Park in the League and a prolonged struggle to get the better of Airdrie in the Scottish Cup seemed to have motivated Jimmy Bissett to try something that he had been considering for some time. On Thursday 27 February, reporter Don John in *The Advertiser* gave everyone a nod and a wink. 'I understand that Dundee are on the track of an experienced forward and are hopeful of

*Alec, shortly after his return to Dundee from Everton in 1930.*

*A cartoon depicting Troup's return to Dundee on 1 March 1930, for a Scottish Cup tie v. Hearts.*

having him fixed up for the cup tie *v.* Hearts.' On Friday, *The Courier* broke the news that it was Alec Troup, and that Mr Bissett and three directors were in Liverpool that day negotiating the transfer.

Everton were easily accommodated, for Troup had not been playing often for them of late. He had been captain for a few games and was still theoretically in that position, but he had not played in the first team for some time. In addition, never having settled his wife and daughter in Liverpool, he was now getting fed up with the travelling and was almost desperate for home, having apparently decided that this was to be his last season with Everton anyway. It may be that Bissett had been informed by some of Troup's friends of his unhappiness, but there is no evidence to suggest that Troup had been 'tapped' or approached illegally before the official enquiry was made.

In this age of hyper-professionalism, astounding wages, grasping agents and sheer unbridled greed, it is perhaps difficult to comprehend that there were (and still are) players who love a club and wish to play for it. 'The only team I ever wanted to play for', is of course a notorious cliché, made infamous by Mo Johnston in 1989 who said it when he was about to sign for Celtic, before he then joined Rangers! But there are occasions in football's history where players play for a team for reasons other than a fast buck. Money came into it, yes, but the heart was more important.

One recalls the famous Tommy McInally of Celtic. He had fallen out with the despotic manager, Maley, and left for Third Lanark, where he plied his reluctant trade for three years. But his heart was ever with Celtic and the phrase 'pining for home' was used to describe his return. Similar phrases could be used about Alec's return to Dundee. When the train reached Perth that Friday evening, the directors waited for a train to Dundee, while Alec continued on the same train to Forfar, having apparently insisted on that point. But he was back in Dundee the following morning by 10.00 a.m. for a light training session and a chance to meet his new team-mates.

This news was a veritable shot in the arm for ailing Tayside. A journalist calling himself 'Unomi' (You know me) in *The Courier* was positively bursting with enthusiasm at the return of Troup, predicting correctly that 'Many will turn up today just to see the wee man'. Hearts were the visitors in the quarter final of the Scottish Cup that Saturday (1 March) and the city almost came to a standstill on Saturday lunchtime as 31,000 scrambled to get to Dens Park to see the second coming of Alec Troup. The old paeans of 'Oh my darling, Eckie Troup' were resurrected as crowds formed at the turnstiles long before the gates were meant to open.

Hearts supporters were also there in their thousands, carrying huge cardboard and wooden hearts with 'Have plenty of this', or 'Don't lose this' inscribed thereon. By coincidence, it had been Hearts who had been the last opponents that Troup had faced for Dundee more than seven years earlier. Now they had a better side, spearheaded by Barney Battles, posthumous son of a previous Barney Battles who had been one of the early Celts. Thousands marched in columns from the station up the centre of the road to Dens Park. *The Courier* was astounded at all this, and could not resist a dig at perceived Edinburgh snobbery: 'We always thought that Hearts fans came to the ground in a chauffeur-driven car.'

George 'Pud' Hill, who himself went on to play for his beloved Dundee in the late 1940s and early 1950s has clear memories of this day, even though he was only eight years old. He recalls the huge crowd, the fact that Dundee had two Everton wingers (Harry Ritchie having joined the club from that source some time previously) and the great reception accorded to Troup. He recalls Troup as being older and balder than he imagined (photographs certainly bear this description out) and remembers the large number of low crosses that Troup sent across at the Provost Road end of the ground.

The team that Alec rejoined was Murray; Brown and Gilmour; McNab, McCarthy and Thomson; Ritchie, O'Hare, Campbell, Robertson and Troup. Troup was cheered every time he touched the ball, although his admirers had to admit that he was a little fatter, a lot balder and appreciably slower than in 1923. This was hardly surprising, for

*Jock Thomson and Alec Troup on a misty day at Dens Park, 1930. Jock would soon be transferred to Everton, where Troup had recently left, and cynics suspected that this was all part of a huge deal.*

he was nearing his thirty-fifth birthday, but the writer in the *Sunday Post* is thrilled by his 'skill in rounding an opponent, his ball control and his accuracy'.

Inspired by Troup, Dundee had a great first half. 'Clap, clap hands here comes Troupie' rang out round the ground as the home side went 2-0 up, and it began to be believed that the Scottish Cup itself was within Dundee's grasp, such is the propensity of human nature to believe anything if desired. 'If we had still had wee Eckie against Celtic yon time …', 'Eh mind o' 1910 … ' Sadly, the euphoria was rudely punctured on two occasions as defensive frailties reared their ugly head once again, and Hearts managed a draw by taking advantage of them.

But interest was still high enough to justify the running of a 'Football Special' to Tynecastle for the replay on the following Wednesday afternoon. Not only that but the *Evening Telegraph* was to run a special late edition – 'on the streets by 5.30 at the latest' – to bring everyone a full-time report on the game. The cash-strapped punters must have got money from such sources as pawning their best suits or selling the family furniture, for 32,000 packed Tynecastle to see the replay – and a large contingent of them were from Dundee.

But it was not to be for the Dundonians. Their defence simply had no answer to the rampant Barney Battles as Hearts scored four. In the forward line, only Troup showed himself to advantage, and even he missed an open goal in the first half, which might have made all the difference. The supporters brooded, but managed to turn out all the clichés like 'it's a blessing in disguise', as the important job was to avoid relegation, and this was really what 'Troupie' had been brought back for.

Dundee did just this (with a degree of comfort), winning their next four home games with Troup scoring in three of them. Only 3,000 saw the Wednesday game on 12 March against Hamilton which Dundee edged 3-2, Troup managing a late winner. There were more the following Saturday to see Troup, 'the master tactician', score twice as Morton were beaten by the same scoreline.

'Everything he did had a masterful air about it. The Forfarian warmed the hearts with skilful runs, deadly centres and goals', said the *Evening Telegraph*.

It was as well that he did this, for Dundee had antagonised their fans once again by selling Jock Thomson before these two vital home games. And where did he go to? Everton! Dundee fans, (and the press) took more than a little convincing that this was not part of the Troup deal, and cynical letters appeared in the local press, concerned that Dundee might soon change their name to Everton Reserves.

But Eckie was back, and with a vengeance. Dispelling any lingering fear of relegation,

*Dundee's forward line against Rangers at Ibrox, 8 August 1931. From left to right: Gavigan, Campbell, Craigie, Robertson, Troup.*

Dundee beat Cowdenbeath and then Ayr United at home to the tune of 3-0. Dundee fans in the mills (or, more likely in that economically disastrous summer of 1930, on the street corners) at last had something to cheer about. The ignominy of relegation had been avoided, but more important, they had their hero back.

They did have other heroes as well in Colin McNab, a fine right half who would go on to win 6 caps for Scotland. Jock Gilmour, the left back would also win an international honour, and there was the legendary goalkeeper Bill Marsh, who was well known for his stentorian voice and organisation of his defence.

For Eckie, there was a sentimental occasion when he was invited to play for Forfar Athletic in a benefit game for Forfar's long-serving stalwart centre half, Allan Smart. Aberdeen, who had two years previously bought Frank Hill from Forfar, provided the opposition. Hill, who would earn his first cap for Scotland a few weeks later, was playing for Aberdeen. Thus, the unique chance was provided at Station Park to see the three Forfarians who had been or would become internationalists – Davie McLean, Alec Troup and Frank Hill. (The veteran Davie McLean was far from finished at this point and had now rejoined Forfar Athletic for the fourth time in his career!) Aberdeen won 1-0, but this was of little concern to the good-natured crowd.

As Alec settled back in Forfar that summer in his small flat, in Stark's Close, beside the lemonade factory, he probably counted himself lucky that he was a professional footballer. Even in Forfar, the ravages of the depression were visible as factory owners and other bosses wickedly took advantage of the situation to cut wages and increase hours, knowing that the workers had no redress other than the dreaded 'dole'. This of course had an effect on trade, particularly on the drapery business, but Alec's shop was still keeping its head above water, if not exactly prospering.

His brother Dave had returned from Canada, although much of the rest of the family were still there. Dave and his family stayed with Alec for a while, and perhaps the idea of going to Canada entered Alec's head as well. But football was in Scotland, and he was back again playing for the team that he loved. Since his return from Everton, Alec now had the option now of travelling by bus to Dundee every day, as bus travel was now becoming more common and was certainly more practical.

*The Courier*, Conservative as always, was enjoying itself by pointing out to its readers (who had disobeyed it by voting Labour the previous year) the shortcomings of Ramsay McDonald's Labour government, which seemed powerless to stop the worsening economic situation. Admiring fingers were even pointed at Italy, where Mussolini had done so much to make trains run on time and workers do a job.

On the sporting front, the Australians were in England again with a young man called Donald Bradman scoring runs prolifically, including a 334 at Headingley. The Duchess of York now had a charming little daughter called Elizabeth, (and after midsummer took up her residence at Glamis Castle awaiting the birth of her second child) and King George V was still around, although his health wasn't that good. And Hitler was that man rising to power in Germany. He was not without his admirers in Britain, but some felt that he was potentially dangerous. However, many assumed that, after the atrocities of the First World War, the Germans would not listen to him.

Dundee started the new season (1930/31) well and with a settled team. Troup, in fact, had the honour of scoring the first goal of the Scottish season, on 9 August against Clyde at Dens Park, as he delighted 12,000 fans with a 'dandy display all-through, tricking his opponents with his old time artistry while his shooting was well on the mark'. He also played in the first-ever First Division game at Bayview, Methil, the following week against East Fife.

The only blot was a narrow 0-1 defeat at the hands of Rangers at Dens Park on 8 August, but *The Courier* is far less concerned with that than the arrival on the scene of a Princess (to be called Margaret) two nights previously. One of the doctors in attendance at Glamis Castle was the Forfar GP, Dr Myles, who arrived back in Forfar in his car, tooting his horn all along the Glamis Road and down West High Street, shouting 'It's a girl!' Disappointment was expressed that it wasn't a boy, (such things were important in these days and in that social circle) but everyone was happy with the event. Forfar hotel keepers played host to the world's press, and decorations and bunting were hung out for the next few days.

The King and the Prince of Wales called in to see the 'chubby-faced' baby en route to Balmoral, where they heard a stern sermon from the minister at Crathie Kirk on the Sunday blaming the economic crisis not on the Labour Government, nor drink but, controversially, on 'men's obsession with sport, which was a misfortune for the country'. One presumes that, given his audience that day, the sport referred to was the supposedly vulgar working-class one of football, rather than more refined and upper-class pursuits like grouse-shooting and fishing!

Be that as it may, the football season continued obsessively and with Dundee playing well. However, on 29 September, a Monday holiday, Dundee were embarrassed – and Troup, one imagines, even more so – by a defeat in the Forfarshire Cup final, at the hands of Forfar Athletic! Nor was there any excuse. The game was at Dens Park, and Dundee were fielding their best team.

They did appear to underestimate the opposition and one or two Dundee players gave the impression that they were not trying all that hard. There was a poor crowd, and it was the Forfar contingent who were delighted at the end when their two goals scored by Davie Kilgour (a Dundonian!) were enough to see them through by 2-1. Troup tried, but seemed unable to inspire the rest of the forward line. Davie McLean was inspirational for Forfar, as was Forfar's goalkeeper Sunter.

No doubt Alec was on the receiving end of some stick from his fellow townsmen after this result. He was as always a consummate professional and any defeat would hurt, even at the hands of Forfar. But there was no great bitterness involved – he even got a lift home that night on the Forfar Athletic bus!

He scored a hat-trick against Ayr United at Somerset Park in November and reports consistently praised the left wing of Alec Troup and his inside man, Jimmy Robertson. For the New Year game at Pittodrie, Dundee took the precaution of travelling up to the Granite City on Hogmanay, the better, one presumes, to keep an eye on errant players who might be inclined to toast the New Year not wisely but well. This would not have affected the teetotal Troup – and in any case it seems to have been a total failure as the Dons beat Dundee 5-1. The local press described this game as a 'dull thud' for Dundee and sang the praises of Aberdeen's Benny Yorston. Significantly, Troup was 'subdued' – which usually meant that Dundee did not play well.

The 1931 Cup campaign got off to a good start when Dundee beat Fraserburgh 10-1, and hit a high spot on 31 January when Dundee went to Ibrox and pulled off a rare triumph. The weather in the east of Scotland was foul – Dundee United's game against Celtic for example was postponed – and snowstorms hit Angus and Fife with a ferocity that *The Courier* found hard to parallel in recent memory. But as so often happens in Scotland, what is snow in the east is rain in Glasgow and this was exactly the case here. If the conditions were anything like as bad as the press implied, then Rangers had cause to complain about the game going ahead. Dundee's first goal, for example, is significantly described as coming when Troup 'got the ball on a dry place and slung it nicely across the goal for Campbell to score'. But Dundee did adapt (Troup in particular) to the wet conditions better than Rangers, and returned home that night to a heroes' welcome in Dundee, a city which was under approximately a foot of snow.

The snow thawed fairly quickly, however, and two weeks later the tie of the round brought Aberdeen to Dens Park. Mindful of their recent thumping at the New Year, Dundee treated their visitors with caution when a wee bit more adventure would have won the day, particularly when Aberdeen lost McMillan with a broken ankle and had, in these pre-substitute days, to play with ten men. The game finished 1-1, and Dundee missed a great chance to win the game when Campbell and Troup left the ball to each other. Forfarian Frank Hill was outstanding for Aberdeen, and a mention is also given to Adam McLean, formerly of Celtic, who had also been one of Troup's rivals for Scotland's left-wing spot in an era when good left wingers seemed to have been plentiful. A Dens Park record of 38,099 saw this game and the Dundee police reported between 800 and 900 cars in the vicinity of the ground.

It was a shame that Dundee did not finish off Aberdeen that day, for they went down 0-2 in the Pittodrie replay which attracted 28,577 on a Wednesday afternoon, 18 February – a day on which there seems to have been more than the usual absenteeism from work with 'influenza', 'granny's funeral' and other mythical problems. Troup hardly rates a mention – the man of the moment is once again Benny Yorston. At one point *The Courier* almost broke with its twee, matronly tradition when it said that 'the trouble with Yorston is that no one can tackle the little beggar properly'.

This more or less finished Dundee's season. Crowds now dipped alarmingly, as did the team's performances. The only moment of note was the well-earned point at Parkhead on 25 March, when Troup's first-time volley to equalise was very significant in depriving Celtic of the League flag. Dundee finished 8th, which was respectable but not enough to inspire the crowds or to bring them back.

The 1931/32 season began on a low note for Dundee, who were thrashed 4-1 at Ibrox. It was a very poor performance, and Rangers (the previous year's Champions) were good, but as far as Troup was concerned, the most important aspect was the beginning of a persecution campaign against him by a journalist in *The Courier*, calling himself 'The Laird'. 'The Laird' said of this game:

> The real disappointment was Alec Troup. It was evident last season that this great personality of the football field was finding League football strenuous. The pace is too hot and after all, Troup has been a long time in the game. Dundee must be on the lookout for a successor to the clever little Forfarian ...

Such criticism stung Alec deeply. He was the first to admit that, at the age of thirty-six, he was slower than of late, but he still believed that he had enough left in him for a season or two. The only way to answer such unfair criticism was on the field, and he showed a determination to prove 'The Laird' wrong. As for Dundee, finding a successor to Troup, there simply was not one available – and in the prevailing economic circumstances of 1931, they certainly had no money to buy one.

Scottish football tried to transcend this general mood of pessimism, but very soon something was to happen to shake the game to its core. On 5 September 1931, Dundee were at Aberdeen. It was a hot, sultry, windless day with (unusually for Pittodrie) no breeze off the sea. The game ended 1-1, and both sides were satisfied with a point apiece. When Alec arrived at Forfar Station, some of the railway men were reading the *Sporting Post*, and Alec asked the results. It was of course 'derby' day, when all the local teams played each other. Forfar Athletic had gone down 0-2 at Arbroath. Alec winced, for he still retained his love of Forfar. Elsewhere, Dundee United had drawn 0-0 with Cowdenbeath and the 'big' game in Glasgow between Rangers and Celtic had resulted in a similar score-line. 'Celtic's goalkeeper goat cerried aff', shouted a railwayman.

Alec was sorry to hear this, for he had played against young John Thomson. He had also met him after games and had been impressed by the sincerity and obvious charm of the young man. Alec hoped the injury wasn't serious for John was well worthy of his place in the Scotland team. He thought little more about it as he hurried home for his tea with Elizabeth and Nan, who had only recently started school.

The following morning, the early editions of the Sunday newspapers contained nothing other than a report on all the games, but the later ones carried the dire tidings that all Glasgow had been plunged into grief late on Saturday night following the death of John Thomson, in the Victoria Infirmary, Langside, Glasgow at 9.25 p.m. Like all professionals and indeed all fans, Alec was distraught. That lithe young man, who had won a Scottish Cup medal only a few months ago to add to his four Scottish caps, was dead! The paper said that it followed a clash with Sam English. Alec knew Sam as well, and felt for him.

In truth, all of Scottish football took some time to recover from this blow.

> The fans they all are silent,
> As they travel near and far,
> No more they'll cheer John Thomson
> That bright and shining star!

But life had to go on, and it did. Alec would nevertheless admit in future years that future games against Celtic had an 'atmosphere' about them, as if what the Celtic supporters were singing had some truth about it.

> So play up Glasgow Celtic,
> Play up and play the game,
> For in your goal a spirit stands,
> Johnny Thomson is its name!

Mercifully, John Thomson, if not unique, is certainly one of the very few footballers to have lost his life as a result of an injury on the football field. It is in this context, however, that we must examine a comment by 'The Laird' on Alec Troup in the derby game against Dundee United the week after the Thomson tragedy.

The game, preceded by a poignant two minute silence, the likes of which was experienced only on Armistice Day, was a poor one. It ended 1-1 and frankly, the football was dreadful. Hardly surprising in the circumstances, perhaps, but 'The Laird' gives Alec his customary round of the guns.

> Why is Troupie so timid? If he had cared, he could have had McIntosh and
> the ball in the net during a second-half raid.

This is a reference to shoulder charging – an act of violence permitted on goalkeepers until the 1950s and exposed for what it was in the 1958 English Cup Final when Nat Lofthouse of Bolton Wanderers bundled the Manchester United goalkeeper over the line and was awarded a goal for it. 'The Laird' seems to think that Troup could have won this particular derby for Dundee in such circumstances.

There are probably four reasons why Alec would not indulge in this. In the first place at 5 ft 5 in, he was hardly the build for it. Secondly, he himself still suffered from his recurrent shoulder problem which he had no desire to aggravate. Thirdly, having stood for two minutes in silence at the tragic death of a goalkeeper a week previously, it was not exactly the time to risk injuring another one. But most of all, this was one aspect of football that the gentle Alec had no time for. He was very competitive and hated losing, believing uncompromisingly that a game of football was there to be won ... but he did not believe in any sort of foul play, even that apparently sanctioned by the Laws.

Troup was ultimately a very nice and a very fair man. Perhaps at times in his career, he could have done with a little more 'devil' in him. He was very proud of his record in never having been 'booked', and, years after his death, his wife would berate her grandson (whose disciplinary record in junior football was less than perfect) with 'Grandie never got booked!'

Dundee's season continued with a mixture of acceptable performances and one or two real shockers. For example, in successive weeks in November, they went to St Mirren and Third Lanark and lost 1-6 on both occasions. And what was significant about these two games? Alec Troup wasn't playing, dropped by manager Jimmy

*Troup shows the press how to take a corner kick before the start of the 1932/33 season for Dundee.*

Bissett, who had clearly been reading 'The Laird' in *The Courier*. A youngster called Monty Monro was given a chance on the left wing on those occasions, but Troup was soon restored.

But there were good days as well, notably the beating of both Celtic and Rangers at Dens Park. On 17 October, with Troup 'reminiscent of his palmy days and waltzing round opponents with consummate ease' (according to 'Don John', not 'The Laird'), Dundee beat a sad, dispirited, melancholic Celtic 2-0, but it was the week before Christmas that really cheered up the troops in the jute factories.

Rangers' defence, Meiklejohn and all, were simply run ragged by a fine Dundee forward line of Gavigan, Smith, Balfour, Campbell and Troup, who won 4-2 on that dark midwinter afternoon of 19 December. Troup played well and even 'The Laird' was compelled to give faint praise: 'inclined to shirk a tackle at first but he too went all out in the end'. However, the hero of the hour was Davie Balfour. Davie, sometimes called 'Conse' for some obscure reason, had Forfar connections as well, having played for Forfar West End before he joined Dundee. That night he was seen to celebrate rather obviously in the West End bar – but no wonder! He remains one of the few centre forwards to have scored a hat-trick against Davie Meiklejohn, something that even the great Jimmy McGrory never achieved.

But Dundee, often described as an 'enigma', came down with another of their 'dull thuds' so beloved by *The Courier* journalists. The following week on Boxing Day, they managed to lose 1-4 at Greenock and although the New Year results (a 0-0 draw against Aberdeen and a 3-0 defeat of Dundee United) were acceptable, they then horrified their fans by losing 0-3 at home to Hamilton Accies on 9 January.

1932 then saw Dundee end up in 10th position in the League, playing poor football in front of miserable crowds, but the biggest downer was the Scottish Cup. It started well with a fine 4-1 win over Morton on 16 January, thereby reversing the Boxing Day disaster. Troup combined well with Robertson, scored the first goal and laid on loads of chances for the rest of the forwards. The next round of the Cup saw Dundee paying a rare visit to Dunfermline.

Dunfermline, even as early as the 1920s, had earned the nickname of The Pars, short for 'paralytic'. Things would be different when Jock Stein took over thirty years later, but at this time Dunfermline were no great shakes, although they had had a good player by the name of Bobby Skinner in the mid-1920s. Moreover, their stadium was notorious for being one of the worst in Scotland, both in terms of playing surface and spectator comfort. For Dundee, although right winger Peter Gavigan was injured, *The Courier* confidently predicted a comfortable victory against the mediocre Fifers who were currently about halfway up the Second Division.

Oh dear! McFadyen scored for Dunfermline early on and, much as Dundee tried, they just could not equalise. Balfour missed several sitters and had an irritating habit of being caught offside. Troup tried hard, but had been the victim of one or two nasty challenges early in the game and Jimmy Robertson deployed perforce on the right wing in the absence of Gavigan was 'no winger', as he himself would cheerfully admit. Dundee had about seventy-five per cent of the pressure, but the full-time whistle came to bring one of the very few rays of sunshine to Dunfermline and further misery for Dundee.

The League was won that year by Motherwell, who thus became the only team other than Celtic or Rangers to win the League between Third Lanark in 1904 and Hibs in 1948. Troup felt that he had played well enough that season. He may have toyed with the idea of retiring, but when offered another one year deal, he accepted it. He was aware of his shortcomings, but he simple loved football too much. 'I'm awfu fond o' fitba', he would say. Before Dundee offered him another year, he might well have been interested in Forfar (or perhaps Brechin) and could have gone part-time to concentrate on his business interests, but no offer came from these quarters

1932/33 was another grim season in Dundee. More jute factories were closing down or on short time and there was little to cheer about on the football field. Troup, now clearly at the veteran stage (he was nearing his thirty-eighth birthday), had lost little of his guile and craft, but was now painfully slow and a lot less sharp on the ball. His speed had never been the factor that drew attention to him, but he had in the past possessed the ability to turn very quickly, and now even that was going. Sometimes, some Dundee fans, forgetful of past glories, turned on Troup, but no more so than they did on others in the team.

In truth it was a very poor Dundee team, which finished 15th out of 20 in the League. Relegation was avoided but only thanks to two home wins late in the season against Kilmarnock and Partick Thistle. A combination of local unemployment and poor football had seen attendance tumble to catastrophic levels. Only 1,500 saw the

*Dundee FC, 1932/33. From left to right, back row: Symon, Morgan, Marsh, Gilmour, McCarthy, Smith. Front row: Munro, Guthrie, Balfour, Robertson, Troup. Scott Symon was an interesting character. Not only did he move on to manage East Fife, Preston North End and Rangers, he was also the first man to be capped for Scotland at both football and cricket.*

game against Kilmarnock on 29 March (admittedly in foul weather), and the average for the season barely reached 5,000. The directors were compelled to announce that not only would they be unable to pay the players their summer 'retainer' fee, but that the staff was going to be pruned in any case.

Troup had been out with an injury over the New Year period, but his return against Clyde on 14 January, where he 'made all the difference', betokened a possible return to winning ways for the team, particularly with the Scottish Cup imminent. A 'run' in the Cup would change things as far as the finances of the club were concerned.

As Dundee disposed of Cowdenbeath in the first round of the Scottish Cup (with a struggle and after a replay) and then Bo'ness in the second, it was foreign affairs that were dominating the headlines, particularly the appointment of Adolf Hitler as Chancellor of Germany. *The Courier* said that he was preferable to Bolshevism, but admitted that he was a very dangerous character. They questioned Hindenburg's reasoning for appointing this dubious character to such a powerful position.

Even further afield, in Australia, things on the cricket field were dominating the sports news. England were winning the Test series, but the Australians were accusing England of being unsportsman-like with their fast bowlers, who seemed to be aiming at the batsman rather than the stumps! The chief target was the captain Douglas Jardine (whose father was Scottish) who encouraged his fast bowler Harold Larwood to employ these 'bodyline' tactics by setting a field to catch rebounds as the Australian batsmen tried to defend themselves! Not only that, but Jardine himself deliberately and provocatively walked out to bat in a Harlequin cap, the very symbol of British imperialism and snobbery.

Such matters would have been discussed (for cricket in the 1930s was very much a topic of working-class conversation) by the none too numerous Dundee supporters as they boarded their special train to take them to Fir Park, Motherwell on 18 February 1933. They knew that this was make or break. A win was essential for the rest of the season, even the future of the club. An unemployed man, who had pawned what little he had to pay the train fare, was still optimistic. 'Eh think it's aw up tae Troupie. He's the man that can dae it for us'. He dolefully reminded everyone however that the victory in the previous round (a 4-0 canter over Bo'ness United) had seen Troup having to leave the field with this shoulder problem again, and this time he had been off for a long time. 'Thae things dunnae get ony easier when ye're aulder, ye ken. My brother had the same problem ... '

Motherwell, of course, were the reigning champions, having won the League in 1932. They still had their great left-wing combination of Stevenson and Ferrier and their manager had Dundee connections. He was, of course, John 'Sailor' Hunter, who had scored the winning goal in 1910 when Dundee won the Scottish Cup. In addition to winning the League in 1932, Motherwell had come within seconds of winning the 1931 Scottish Cup Final against Celtic until they conceded an own goal, of all things! They were a fine side.

This game in February 1933 was a total disaster for Dundee. It all hinged on an incident with wing half Scot Symon. Symon, a local man from Errol in Perthshire who had joined Dundee from the local junior side Dundee Violet, would have a massive influence on Scottish sport in later years. He has the distinction of being the first man to win a cap for Scotland at both football and cricket. He played for Rangers and then went on to manage them in their golden Baxter-inspired years of the early 1960s. He was also the man who built up the great East Fife team of the post-war era which won three League Cups from 1947 to 1953, and was the manager of Preston North End when they unluckily lost the 1954 FA Cup final.

But this was one of Symon's less happy occasions. He was sent off as Dundee crashed out 0-5 to a rampant Motherwell team. *The Courier* admitted that it was a tough tackle, but said 'the pointing to the pavilion by the referee' surprised onlookers. Dundee were already in arrears, and after that there was no way back for them. Troup tried hard but he was 'watched like a hawk', with Motherwell able to use their numerical advantage to deploy an extra man on him.

This was a sad game for Troup for two reasons. One was that it destroyed any lingering chance he had of ever winning a Scottish Cup medal, something that he

123

*Alec taking his dog for a walk, not long after announcing his retirement from the game in 1933.*

would have cherished, but also because it was probably this game which determined that there would be no 'next season' for Troup at Dens Park. The club, in huge debt and still labouring to pay off the new stand built over ten years previously, simply could not afford to retain the ageing and injury-prone Troup.

His last game for the club was against Celtic on 22 April 1933. Celtic had won the Cup the previous week, beating Motherwell 1-0 in a dull final, but their League form had been poor. Even a vague suggestion in the press that Celtic might bring the Scottish Cup with them to show off to their many fans in the Dundee and Angus area (they didn't as it turned out!) or the chance to see Jimmy McGrory, who had scored a great goal for Scotland against England at Hampden three weeks previously (he was injured, in any case) failed to entice more than 10,000 to see them.

Nor did anyone know (possibly not even Troup himself) that this would be Troup's last big game for Dundee. The game was something of an anti-climax, played on a dry bumpy pitch against opposition who were resting on their laurels with the Scottish Cup in the bag and who had given up for the season. Dundee won 3-0, which at least gave their fans something to cheer about. Bobby Hogg, Celtic's right back, 'failed to put a stopper on Troup. His crosses were all stamped 'gilt-edged', said *The Courier*. The team was Marsh, Morgan and Gilmour; Symon, McCarthy and Blyth; Smith, Guthrie, Robertson, Miller and Troup.

Troup didn't play in the last League game against East Stirling on 29 April. It was a dismal occasion in any case, with Dundee losing 2-3 to the already relegated East Stirling. But Troup had a tremendous recompense. A few midweek phone calls ensured a ticket for him at the greatest football occasion of the season – the FA Cup final of Everton *v.* Manchester City at Wembley! A hat-trick for his old friend Dixie Dean guaranteed the first Everton Cup victory since 1906. Alec was delighted for Dixie and the rest of the Everton team, quite a few of whom he still knew, but he must have regretted that he was not out there on the field with them! His otherwise brilliant career missed the privilege of playing a big game at Hampden or Wembley. But he must have smiled at the sight of his fellow 'Forfarian', The Duchess of York, handing over the trophy to his great friend Dixie.

He was possibly still hoping against hope for a re-engagement with Dundee the following season, for he still loved the game. But he was now thirty-eight, and he noted that his old rival for the Scotland spot, Alan Morton, had announced his retirement. Any slight chance he might have had went when manager Jimmy Bissett resigned in the early part of the close season, and was replaced by the former Rangers full back Billy McCandless. Billy understandably wanted to sweep clean with a new broom, and Alec was not offered terms.

Thus with a whimper came to an end the playing career of Alec Troup. Being the provident soul that he was, Alec had long considered other ways of earning a living. The money that he had earned from Everton (by no means a king's ransom, but enough in the context of the 1920s and 1930s) had allowed him to invest in the purchase of his gentleman's outfitter shop in Castle Street, Forfar, and now he could consolidate and diversify that business. At the end of summer 1933, advertisements which appeared in the *Forfar Dispatch* for the Corner Hat and Cap Shop at 26 Castle Street run by

A. Troup also boasted that it sold Jantsen Swimming Costumes (the last word in summer luxury) and other articles of clothing.

But had his career really come to an end? Rumours spread round Forfar that Troup might yet be enticed back by James Black to play another year or two with Forfar Athletic. After all, Davie McLean had continued until he was forty-two, and Troup was 'only' thirty-eight! There is a certain indication that the matter was at least discussed between Black and Troup, but if any offer was made, Troup's answer, in spite of his continuing love for the game and indeed for Forfar Athletic, was 'No'.

There were good reasons for this. Troup had been lucky enough to avoid any career-threatening injury (his brow did bear the mark of a stud caused by an accidental collision, but this did not affect him playing) but he was now aware that he was struggling more than he used to with thigh, groin and ankle strains as well as the occasional attack of sciatica in his left leg. It was better to quit while the going was good.

Oddly enough, his shoulder problem did not bother him all that much. It did occur frequently, but it could be easily righted. It was more painful now when it did happen, however. Moreover, he was very aware that it was a young man's game. He had seen too many people of his own age going on for too long. He did not want the cheers to turn to jeers. He was also aware of the old adage about retirement that you should go when people still asked 'Why?' and before they began to say 'Why not?' A dignified retiral was therefore in order.

Not that it was easy for him. He had played professional football for almost twenty years (and even his break in the army had seen quite a lot of football) and although he still had his trade as a plasterer in addition to his business interests of a draper's shop, he was very aware that he had had little experience of life apart from football.

But he managed with the help of his family, and there was little doubt as to his main topic of conversation. On a Saturday afternoon he would frequently be seen watching Forfar Athletic or if they were away from home, at one or other of the Junior teams, particularly Forfar Celtic or Forfar North End, for whom he retained an affection. He, like many other ex-professionals, no doubt found it frustrating to watch, but he learned to cope. He played in a charity match in April 1934 for Dundee *v.* Perth at Muirton Park. On the other side was Alan Morton!

He would have been very concerned about the European political situation. Troup, like many an ex-serviceman, came home not so much burning with patriotic fervour as determined that he and his family should never see the same thing again. Yet this was precisely what was happening. The Italians invasion of Abyssinia, a ferocious civil war in Spain from 1936 and Hitler's rule in Germany showed that fascism was gaining increasing strength in Europe.

This did have one beneficial side effect as far as the jute industry in the Angus area was concerned. The government was rightly concerned about aerial warfare and the horrendous effects of bombing. The First World War had introduced the world to the concept of 'civilian casualties', and any future war was going to be worse. Something, however, that could cushion the effect of bombs was sand bags, and for these they needed jute ... and in great quantities. From about 1935 onwards, the factories of Dundee and Forfar were enjoying a previously unheard of boom, with lots of overtime. The depression was over – but at what cost?

Social life in Forfar was now centred on two cinemas – the Pavilion (which had now outlasted Shand's and was commonly referred to as the 'Gaffie'), and the Regal, a palatial looking place in East High Street. Both cinemas, which lasted well into the 1960s before dismally surrendering to bingo, boasted from the early 1930s onwards that they had 'talkie' facilities and that the woman who played the piano in chases or love scenes was no longer necessary. Hollywood came to Forfar in a big way, and Saturday night would see two 'hooses' at the pictures as Errol Flynn, Humphrey Bogart, Merle Oberon and Heddie LeMarr became the celluloid role models of the new age. However, the new leaders in Germany would not be quietened.

# 9
# SCOTLAND

Until very recently in Scottish footballing history, the greatest thing that one could do was to play for one's country. The pulling of the dark blue shirt of Scotland over one's shoulders was what everyone dreamed of. Talk of a 'cap' for a particular player was the main topic of conversation of every supporter. In the 1920s, given the absence of World Cups and foreign opposition, the Home International Championship as it was called – competed for by Scotland, England, Wales and Ireland (as they were then still called) – was very important, and in particular the fixture against England was looked forward to and much relished. It was the highlight of the season.

The contrast with today could not be more marked. The World Cup still does manage to whip up a certain amount of enthusiasm as it comes round every four years, as does the European Championship, but the Home International Championship has long gone – a victim, one feels with a touch of sadness, of sheer greed in that playing for one's club in a European tournament seems to generate so much more money and interest.

Today, we have the predictable and annoying spectacle of players suddenly becoming injured a few days before an International, and more than one superstar has admitted years later that his club 'encouraged' him to do so, as if this was not obvious in any case to the fans! This attitude began as early as the 1960s, with the spread of European club competitions. It also appears that certain stars seemed to perform a lot less well for Scotland than they did for their clubs. The finger might be pointed at quite a few 'heroes' of English clubs who distinctly underperformed at International level for Scotland. It is a sad fact that the Scottish admirers of men like Denis Law and Kenny Dalglish have often felt short-changed.

Not that it applied only to Scotland. The author remembers an encounter on a train one night with the late Don Revie, sometime manager of Leeds United and later of England. Don was charming and pleasant and he freely admitted to faking a few injuries for his players when he was manager of Leeds United, but also to being very annoyed when it was done to him as manager of England by several managers of clubs whom he knew to be lying through their teeth as they talked about hamstrings, Achilles tendons and pulled muscles. One well known manager was more honest, saying 'The boy could do with a rest'!

Such an attitude would have appalled Alec Troup and anyone else of his generation. In fact, it still appalls certain people of a slightly younger age, for whom playing for Scotland remains more or less the be-all and end-all of football existence. But it is sadly true that money talks louder than patriotism.

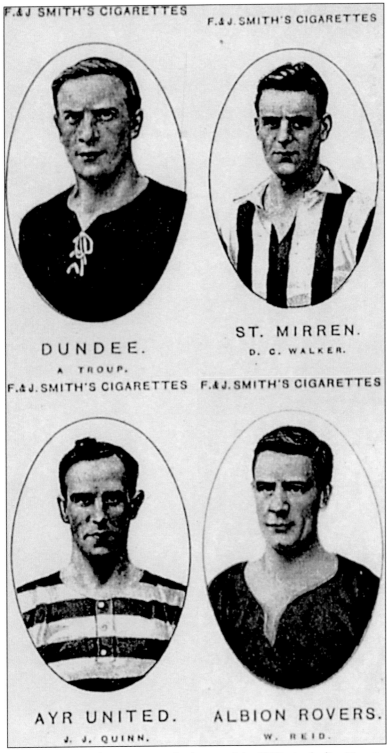

*Cigarette cards showing Scottish players of the 1920s, including Troup.*

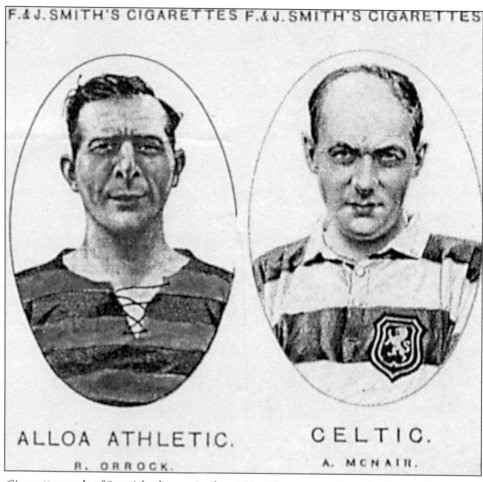

F.&J. SMITH'S CIGARETTES F.&J. SMITH'S CIGARETTES

ALLOA ATHLETIC.        CELTIC.

R. ORROCK.        A. McNAIR.

*Cigarette cards of Scottish players in the 1920s. The one on the right shows Alec's great friend and adversary, Alec McNair of Celtic.*

People may well ask why, if Alec Troup was so good, he only won five full international 'caps' for Scotland and two League 'caps' (i.e. for the Scottish League). The answer is simple – Alan Lauder Morton. Arguments continued to rage throughout Troup's life about the relative merits of both men, but most historians seem to agree that Morton was a shade faster and more direct. A contemporary source says however that 'although lacking the pace of Morton, Troup has coolness, keenness and a host of wiles, and in squaring a ball, he has few equals'. In addition, Alan Morton never played badly for Scotland. Playing for Rangers (as he did after 1920) may also have been a factor, although Troup himself was always careful to distance himself from any allegations of bias.

There was also Adam McLean of Celtic, a grossly underrated player in the eyes of Parkhead historians. However, he was not quite in the same bracket as Troup or Morton. Yet, he was given the nod on three occasions in preference to Troup when Morton was unavailable. He performed adequately too, it must be said.

Following the First World War, internationals resumed in the season of 1919/20. Scotland drew in Wales in February 1920 and then went on to beat Ireland handsomely at Parkhead in March. On both occasions, Morton (still, until summer 1920, an amateur with Queen's Park) was on the left wing and he played well. Troup, therefore, although playing consistently well for Dundee, could hardly complain about not being selected. *The Courier* might moan about such things and how players in provincial teams were often overlooked, but that was the way life was.

A chance would be given to habitues of Dens Park on 27 March 1920 to compare the two men, for Queen's Park were due to appear at Dens Park. The game ended 1-1 and most supporters would agree that the Troup *v.* Morton contest also ended in a draw, with both men playing well. Morton, however, seemed to pick up a knock in a clash with Dundee's makeshift centre half, Dave 'Roy' McDonald. He was called 'Roy' to distinguish him from the other Dave McDonald who also played for Dundee at the time. 'Roy' was nothing more than a fringe player and his Dundee career was fairly insignificant – apart from the indirect effect of his accidental collision with Alan Morton.

The England game, as always, was the big one and this year it was scheduled for Saturday 10 April at Sheffield. Troup had been selected for the international trial, Home Scots *v.* Anglo-Scots at Cathkin Park on Wednesday 30 March, along with Napper Thomson of Dundee and against former Dundonian John Paterson, now with Leicester City. The 'dapper Forfar outside left', as *The Courier* dubbed Troup, played brilliantly that afternoon, but it was still no great surprise that the consistent Alan Morton, although rested for the trial in view of his knock at Dens Park, retained his place for the big game.

*The Courier* was somewhat mollified in its anger by the consoling news that John Paterson was picked for the inside left spot. John was an interesting character, having been wounded no less than five times while serving with the Black Watch in the First World War. He had only recently gone from Dundee to Leicester for a large four-figure sum. Cynics suspected that the transfer was something to do with the projected financing of the new obtuse-angled stand being planned on the north side of Dens Park, but John was still a Dundonian and well-loved by the supporters. They were delighted to hear the news that he had been picked for Scotland.

Troup was naturally disappointed when the team was announced on 31 March, the day after his fine game at Cathkin. But Alan Morton did not play for Queen's Park against Partick Thistle on 3 April, nor against Morton (of Greenock!) on 5 April, nor Kilmarnock on 7 April, and rumours circulated to the effect that the injury sustained at Dens Park was serious. These rumours intensified, fuelled by press speculation. On the morning of Thursday 8 April 1920, a telegram arrived at Dens Park for Mr Alexander Troup. During the war years, telegrams had usually been bad news. This one was very good!

Troup had to be in Glasgow on Friday at 10.00 a.m for the train down to Sheffield. He was congratulated by his Dundee team-mates and Manager Sandy MacFarlane, and the reporter of *The Courier* who had arrived at Dens Park for his routine morning call had a scoop. News travelled fast to Forfar and, by mid-afternoon, people talked about

F.&J. SMITH'S CIGARETTES

ABERDEEN.

J. MILLER.

*J. Miller was one of the Scottish players of the 1920s. Prior to the Second World War, Aberdeen wore black and gold vertical stripes, rather than red.*

little other than 'Troupie' getting a cap for Scotland against England. He was not, of course, the first Forfarian to do so, for Davie McLean had achieved this honour in 1912, but it was still a very proud moment for the dazed Mrs Christina Troup. Only two short years before, she had spent many sleepless nights worrying about what was happening 'ower thair' in France and Belgium and now she had a son playing for Scotland against England in the first official post-war international betweeen the two countries. How his father would have enjoyed this, she thought!

*The Courier* put to one side any parochial considerations like Ayr United *v.* Dundee or Airdrie *v.* Raith Rovers and turned its total attention to the international, in particular the 'all-Dundee' left wing of Paterson and Troup. Implying that the two men had not always got on well together in the past, in a football sense at least (in fact they had played together only once before!), the hope was expressed that they would 'knit together', for the game depended on them! There was of course other local interest for Andy Wilson the centre forward was currently playing for Dunfermline Athletic.

Troup was understandably very nervous as he travelled down on the train that Friday along with the other Home Scots. Rain was falling heavily and persistently, and fears were being expressed in the Press that the pitch might resemble a 'gluepot'. The gentlemanly Alec McNair of Celtic, whom Troup had always liked, was sensitive to the situation and made a point of playing cards with the debutant, of telling stories and jokes and expressing the hope that this would be the first appearance of a long and successful Scotland career.

Some of the Anglo-Scots who joined the rest of the party at the Royal Victoria Hotel were unfamiliar to Troup, who was a little overawed in such exalted company, but he needn't have been, for they were very supportive and helpful. In particular the 'Laughing Cavalier', Wilfrid Low of Newcastle, who was an Aberdonian and been to Forfar 'aince an nae for lang', was very friendly.

Playing for Scotland was a social occasion in those days. Dinner would be served in

*Alec in 1920, soon after winning his first Scottish cap. Observe the 'orange slice' type of ball.*

the hotel only to those who were wearing a collar and tie, and any drunken or anti-social behaviour would be rewarded with the first train home and no further consideration under any circumstances for an international 'cap'. In addition, trips were arranged for the Sunday after the game. The team went sightseeing in the neighbouring Peak District, with a trip to the Speedwell Cavern mine being the highlight. It is not recorded whether the players enjoyed these experiences or not.

Sheffield 'the cutlery town' was thriving in the immediate post-war years. Like many other places, it had suffered dreadfully in terms of numbers of young men lost, but it was fighting back. The town itself had done very well during the war out of the munitions industries which had taken over local factories to make metal plates for tanks and other war necessities. Although the invasion of Scottish fans in 1920 was nothing like as extensive as it would become to Wembley in later decades, there was still a sizeable Scottish presence on that rainy day in Sheffield.

The charabanc run to Bramall Lane was a nervous affair with butterflies in the stomach, but there was also a certain amount of adrenalin as well. Pulling on the Scotland jersey was, as Davie McLean had told him before the war, the greatest feeling one could experience. But then the worldly-wise Davitt paused and added lecherously: 'In fact, tae be honest, Eckie, it's only the second best feelin'!'

It was another Forfar voice, however, that calmed Alec down in the corridor at Bramall Lane. 'Keep the heid noo, Eckie, keep the heid'. 'Jeem' Black, his mentor at Forfar Athletic before the war, was now sufficiently 'weel in' with the SFA to wangle a free trip to watch Scotland. It was so reassuring to hear a familiar voice, and he was similarly happy to look around and see the more experienced internationals like Alec McNair and Jimmy Gordon equally on edge.

The preliminaries took an age and Alec was glad to hear the referee's whistle to start the match on a muddy spongy park – the sort of surface which occasionally suited Troup, although it did make it difficult to cross the ball. The last time he had seen conditions like this, Alec thought soberly, had been on the killing fields of the First World War. How lucky he was to have escaped all that – and to be playing now for his country! It was difficult to comprehend why he had been so lucky.

The teams on Saturday 10 April 1920 were:

England: Hardy (Liverpool), Longworth (Liverpool) and Pennington (West Bromwich Albion); Ducat (Aston Villa), McCall (Preston North End) and Grimsdell (Tottenham Hotspur); Wallace (Aston Villa), Kelly (Burnley), Cock (Chelsea), Morris (West Bromwich Albion) and Quantrill (Derby County).

Scotland: Campbell (Liverpool); McNair (Celtic) and Blair (Sheffield Wednesday); Bowie (Rangers), Low (Newcastle United) and Gordon (Rangers); Donaldson (Bolton Wanderers), Miller (Liverpool), Wilson (Dunfermline Athletic), Paterson (Leicester City) and Troup (Dundee).

Referee – Mr T. Dougray, Belshill.

It was a remarkable game which ended 5-4 for England – Kelly scored two for England and Cock, Morris and Quantrill one each, and Scotland replied with two from Miller and one each from Donaldson and Wilson. Troup played well throughout, particularly in the first half where he was described as a 'box of tricks' against Ducat and Longworth – a point graciously and magnanimously conceded by England's captain Ducat in the post-match interview. Ducat had never seen Troup before, and like the rest of the 50,000 Yorkshire crowd, he was mightily impressed, saying that 'the little chap had the heart of a lion'.

The result might have been different if Scotland (whose players tended to be of a slighter build than the Englishmen) had not tired in the second half (after being ahead 4-2 at half-time). The defence made quite a few blunders, with Alec McNair at right back and goalkeeper Kenny Campbell being particularly blameworthy. Campbell's career was in a strange phase at that moment, for he had been replaced as Liverpool's goalkeeper by Hardy, who was in the opposite goal for England that day! Campbell was in the throes of moving back to Scotland to Partick Thistle, with whom he would win a Scottish Cup medal the following year. Today was not one of Kenny's better days.

John Paterson, the much-vaunted Dundonian at inside left, struggled to make any great impact on the game, but Troup was 'the star of the left side of the park'. Indeed, in the dying minutes, Troup beat his man and shot from the edge of the box, only to see the ball strike the post. Moments like these are quite definitive. Had that ball hit the post and rebounded into the net, Troup would have deservedly been a hero for gaining a draw for Scotland in this high-scoring international. As it was, Eckie had the chagrin of seeing the ball rebound to an English defender.

Back in Forfar, a posse of folk eager for news of the game gathered at the Post Office, for Jim Black had promised to send a telegram. A rumour (correct, as it turned out) had reached the town from the Sporting Post office in Dundee that Scotland were 4-2 up at half time. There was of course no television nor radio in those days, but the anticipation experienced in Castle Street that afternoon was second to none. How had 'wee Troupie' done? In the event the telegram came at about 5 o'clock with the score 'England 5 Scotland 4' and underneath the laconic statement 'Scotland unlucky – Troup good'. It was in fact a fair summing up of the game.

The papers the next day and on the Monday gave more details. *The Athletic News*, a mid-week paper said: 'Troup was the prettiest kind of a player, with plenty of cunning in either foot. At his best in the first half, he was really responsible for opportunities which yielded three goals, and no man could wish to do more either in his first or his tenth international match.'

*The Courier*'s Special Correspondent was jubilant:

> Troup delighted Sheffield people. "Who's Troup?" they were asking
> on Saturday morning but well they know who Troup is now and what
> he can do. Alec amazed everybody by the neat, fast way he scampered
> through the Hillsborough mud, also by his accurate crossing and shooting
> abilities, to say nothing of the dance he led Ducat and the clean heels he
> showed Longworth.

But the *Forfar Dispatch* had its own eulogy to Forfar's greatest son. The very erudite David Mackie, teacher of English at Forfar Academy (who would go on to write a book called *Forfar in the Great War*) wrote under the pseudonym of 'The Drummer'. This title was, of course, in remembrance of the way in which news was spread around the town a century previously before local newspapers were thought of. Mackie would write until his death in 1933, when the pseudonym was adopted by someone else. In April 1920, there appears a poem by The Drummer called 'Eckie Homo' – homo being the Latin word for a man and Eckie a deliberate corruption of the Latin word 'ecce' meaning 'look' as in 'Ecce Romani' – Look, the Romans!

Eckie Homo
Gin ony unco body speer
Wha sets a Farfar herts asteer
And cock-a-hoop,
Juist whisper i' the body's ear,
Wee Eckie Troup!

In Sheffield whar, like bees in hives
The fowks a' cutlers cutling knives
Or spuins for soup,
They've got the sharpening o their lives
Frae Eckie Troup!

*Scotland v. Wales, 12 February 1921. This was Pittodrie's first ever international, and in the background is the Beach End. The players are, from left to right, back row: McMullan, Harris, Pringle, Cunningham, McStay, Marshall. Front row: Archibald, Wilson, Campbell, Cassidy, Troup.*

C-3 ye'd think him frae his length:
For grit and guts and kickin strength
A-1's his group;
Ye shuid a seen him on the tenth
Wee Eckie Troup!

Like ilka honest Farfar loon
(A in a circle like) stand roun
And pass the stoup:
Gin there's a drappie, drink it doun
Tae Eckie Troup!

The terms A-1 and C-3 show that the poem was written in the aftermath of war. A-1 was the description given to a soldier in first-class condition after a medical test. Posters encouraging soldiers to be fit would often say 'B 1 of those soldiers who are A-1'. C-3 were those unfit for military duty.

The Biblical quotation about a prophet being without honour in his home town clearly did not apply to Alec Troup in 1920! Forfar folk, with all their losses and sufferings during that terrible war and now back in the dreadful jute factories, clearly needed a hero. They now most certainly had one!

Troup's next international outing was in the following season for the Scottish League against the Irish League. These internationals are no longer played nowadays, but were very important until the early 1960s, after which their importance declined steeply. Players eligible were those who played football in the Scottish League, whether they were Scottish-born or not. Patsy Gallacher, for example, Celtic's immensely talented Irishman, picked up two Scottish League caps in 1913 and 1924.

The first Scottish League appearance however was in early 1921, after the game against the Irish League at Ibrox had been put off because of fog on 27 October 1920, something which caused immense disappointment to the two Dundee players in the party namely Alec Troup and centre half Dyken Nicoll, also coincidentally a Forfar man. The game was rescheduled for 25 January 1921 at Ibrox. The team, of course, had to be picked again, and although Dyken would have been grievously disappointed to be dropped in favour of St Mirren's Pringle, Dundee had compensation in the re-selection of Troup and the elevation to the left-back spot of Napper Thomson.

Scottish weather is usually at its worst around about Burns night (it certainly was in 1759 with its 'blast o' Januar wind' which 'blew hansel in on Robin') and it was grim in 1921. But in spite of widespread fears of another postponement, the snow melted in Glasgow sufficiently for the referee, Mr Jackson, to sanction play, although there was residual fog around. Thus 20,000 people were able to see the Scottish League thump their Irish counterparts by 3-0. The outstanding success for Scottish League was the left-wing pairing of Joe Cassidy and Alec Troup. Alec was 'spoon-fed' by Joe and the result was electric.

Even the Glasgow crowd, although the occasional Dundonian voice was also heard in the main stand shouting for 'Napper' and 'Troupie' (according to *The Dundee*

*Advertiser*), were enthralled by this performance. Troup had a hand in the other two goals and could be credited with the third. He hit a low powerful shot from the edge of the box, which Mehaffy at full length could not quite hold and Rankine tapped in the rebound.

The teams were:

Scottish League: Robb (Rangers), Hamilton (Kilmarnock) and Thomson (Dundee), Gilchrist (Celtic), Pringle (St Mirren) and McMullan (Partick Thistle), Archibald (Rangers), Rankine (Motherwell), French (Morton), Cassidy (Celtic) and Troup (Dundee).

Irish League: Mehaffy; McSweney and Ferguson (all Glentoran); Watson (Shelbourne), Scraggs (Glentoran), Harris (Cliftonville); McGregor and Crooks (both Glentoran), Scott (Linfield), Meek (Glentoran) and Jackson (Cliftonville).

Alec did not travel back to Forfar that night but stayed on in Glasgow with his friend Dyken Nicholl (who had clearly recovered from his disappointment at being dropped for the re-run of the game). They went to a show in Glasgow that night, and then the following day went to see a Cup replay at Airdrie, where the home side went down 0-1 to Clyde. They also spent some time with the Irish lads before they sailed the following day.

Troup could not help but admire these Irishmen. Their country had been in civil war since the end of the First World War, newspapers carried daily reports of atrocities carried out by Sinn Fein and the barbaric Black and Tans, recruited from Dartmoor and Peterhead prisons for no other reason than their brutality, yet here they were playing football, cheerful as ever – and no one seeemd to care who was a Protestant and who was a Catholic. Watson, for example, was from the South, Jackson from Catholic Cliftonville, Scott from the Orange Linfield. Yet there they were eating and drinking happily together in spite of all that and a 0-3 drubbing from the Scots! The reason was that they loved their football. There was a lesson there, thought Troup, who had already begun to form a worthy detestation of the religious hatred so evident whenever Dundee played either Celtic or Rangers.

Troup retained his place for the next full Scottish international. This was against Wales at Pittodrie on 12 February 1921 and Scotland won 2-1. The retention of Troup was expected, for he had continued his sparkling form for Dundee, a feature being the understanding that he had struck up with Johnny Bell, the centre forward whose prolific goalscoring owed much to Alec Troup. Dundee were having a good season and even felt strong enough to excuse Troup from a routine League match against lowly Clydebank the Wednesday before the international, lest Alec injure himself. This move, which did Dundee a great deal of credit, showed the importance they attached to having one of their own men playing for Scotland and contrasts sharply with the attitude of some clubs today!

Internationals against Wales and Ireland were not, of course, considered as important as the big one against England, but they were still mighty occasions. The

Wales game was a particularly important game in the history of Aberdeen. The club was only formed in 1903 and here was Pittodrie being asked for the first time to host a Scotland international fixture. The crowd was 22,000 and the stadium was 'well-filled but not overcrowded' and a little short of the record attendance of 25,000. However, the receipts were a healthy £2,400.

Troup would have had quite a few of his friends and relatives taking the train from Forfar to see the game, one would imagine, but the writer of *The Scotsman* felt that Troup had played better. ' ... he was not as good as he normally is in "big" football, and he and Cassidy were poor as a wing, although the fault lay mainly with Cassidy.' This was in contrast to the recent League international against the Irish League, where Alec had linked very well with Celtic's Joe Cassidy. Another report states that 'Troup's crosses were poor. As a rule he sent them over badly, either too square or behind the other forwards'.

Yet 'facts are chiels that winnae ding' as the Ayrshire poet put it and it was Troup who sent over the cross for Andy Wilson to score the winner. Scotland did win 2-1 and won well. The selectors clearly had not read what the scribe of *The Scotsman* said, for Cassidy and Troup were retained for the next game. Troup gave an interview to *The Courier* following the Pittodrie game in which he expressed his satisfaction with what had happened, but felt that he could have 'done with more of the ball'.

The teams were:

Scotland: Campbell (Partick Thistle), Marshall (Middlesbrough) and McStay (Celtic), Harris (Partick Thistle), Pringle (St Mirren) and McMullan (Partick Thistle); Archibald (Rangers), Cunningham (Rangers), Wilson (Dunfermline), Cassidy (Celtic) and Troup (Dundee).

Wales: Peers (Wolverhampton Wanderers), Millership (Rotherham) and Russell (Plymouth Argyle), Keenor (Cardiff City), Jones (Swansea Town) and Mathias (Wrexham); Williams (Merthyr Tydfil), Collier (Grimsby Town), Hoddinot (Watford), Davies (Preston North End) and Vizard (Bolton Wanderers).

Referee – Mr Mason of Burslem.

The next international came along two weeks later on 26 February 1921 and it was at Windsor Park, Belfast. It was a game not without its danger, for Ireland was in turmoil in the early months of 1921, as the South demanded freedom from Britain and the North refused. Violence, either from the IRA or the Black and Tans or the various Ulster groups, was an everyday occurrence.

Troup must have felt that he was heading into a war zone as the Scottish team assembled at the Broomielaw in Glasgow for the crossing. In the case of many of the players, it was not the first time that they had embarked on a ship heading for a war zone, and it must have brought back memories of comrades who had sailed on a ship with them but had not returned.

In the event, the game passed very peacefully and Scotland won comfortably 2-0.

The teams were:

Ireland: Scott (Liverpool), Mulligan( Manchester City) and Rollo (Blackburn Rovers); Lacey (Liverpool), Smith (Cardiff City) and O'Brien (Queen's Park Rangers); McGregor (Glentoran), Ferris (Chelsea), McKinney (Hull City), Hamill (Manchester City) and Bookman (Luton Town).

Scotland: Campbell (Partick Thistle), Marshall (Middlesbrough) and McStay (Celtic); Harris (Partick Thistle), Graham (Arsenal) and McMullan (Partick Thistle); McNab (Morton), Miller (Manchester United), Wilson (Dunfermline Athletic), Cassidy (Celtic) and Troup (Dundee)

Referee – Mr Ward of Kirkham.

There were several things worthy of mention about this game, not unconnected with the Troubles. One was the huge presence of the military, who were on hand to prevent any disturbances, although it was difficult not to believe that their actual presence did add to the feeling of menace. At a Gaelic football game in Dublin, soldiers had actually opened fire on the crowd. Another noticeable thing was the reaction of the crowd every time Ferris or Hamill touched the ball. These men now played for English clubs but had recently moved from Belfast Celtic, and therefore were booed by the partisan Linfield-supporting crowd. McStay and Cassidy of Glasgow Celtic received similar treatment, but that it less surprising because they were the opposition, after all!

Yet another factor worthy of questioning is why there were no Rangers players in either team. Sandy Archibald, Andy Cunningham and Alan Morton might well have been picked for Scotland, and Billy McCandless for Ireland. In Morton's case, Dundonians and Forfarians would of course say that Troup was better, but it was less easy to defend the exclusion of the other three. Was this some deliberate policy on the part of Rangers to keep their players away from such a troublesome fixture? Rangers were playing a Scottish Cup tie that day – but it was a replay against Alloa at Ibrox, hardly the most demanding of fixtures. Moreover, although McStay and Cassidy of Celtic played for Scotland, why was the prodigious Patsy Gallacher not playing for Ireland?

This was clearly a very abnormal International, and another surreal touch was applied when Scotland came out, not in dark blue, but in white with black pants, looking for all the world like England! It is of course not unknown in the modern world to have bizarre changes of kit for commercial reasons to do with sponsors, or even to avoid an apparent clash of colours as far as television is concerned, but this decision in 1921 defies any sort of explanation. It was not even as if blue and green would have looked similar on monochrome television! Thirty or forty years would pass before this became a consideration.

*The Scotsman*, most unusually for an Edinburgh paper catering for the bourgeoisie, devoted a great deal of space to this game and was very enthusiastic about Scotland's performance. (This is in contrast to the Scottish rugby team, who disgraced themselves rather badly in Dublin that same day.) In particular, Alec Troup was singled out. 'Troup made Lacey , the Irish captain look very small' ( a reference to the way Troup played rather than their comparative height, one feels, for Lacey was a good six inches taller than the diminutive 5 ft 5 in Eckie) and 'Truly, we had a great outside left,' said the newspaper. If Alec had read *The Scotsman*, he would have enjoyed the 'we', for small-town men like Troup occasionally felt excluded by the urbane city slickers, particularly from Edinburgh, with its not entirely undeserved reputation for snobbery.

Both goals came from Troup. It was Troup's cross which resulted in a handling offence for Andy Wilson to score the penalty, and Joe Cassidy's fine strike was a result of him being released by Troup's visionary inside pass. Not only that, but Troup himself scored a third goal, disallowed for reasons that the press said were 'mystifying' and 'peculiar'. It was noticeable at the end that the Scottish soldiers in the excessive military presence made a point of shaking Troup's hand as he ran off the park.

Troup had every reason to be proud of himself, and the press confidently predicted the same team for England on 9 April at Hampden. Granted, the opposition had been poor and the circumstances unusual, but the team had played well. Troup continued to perform well for Dundee, who had a good season, and it was therefore all the more of a disappointment to see when the team was announced that the left wingers were not Cassidy and Troup but the Rangers pair of Andy Cunningham and Alan Morton.

This was not before some bizarre happenings at Cathkin Park on 22 March. It was normal practice for there to be a game between Home Scots and Anglo Scots – a sort of international trial game. Troup was picked – but for the Anglo Scots! This was to give Morton a game with the Home Scots, so that the selectors could compare them. As the newspapers rightly pointed out, this tended to cut the feet from under the idea of Home Scots *v.* Anglo Scots, but events were compounded by Morton's withdrawal through illness. Troup was thus promoted to the Home Scots team – and his replacement in the Anglo Scots was Adam McLean of Celtic (who were not exactly an English team either!) For the record, the Home Scots won 2-1, and it is just possible that Troup did himself no favours with a performance which even his apologists in the Dundee press described as 'good, but not all that great'.

Be that as it may, the choosing of the Rangers pair for the left wing spots for the game against England was controversial to say the least. Admittedly, both Rangers were having a good season, but it was a decision that smacked of favouritism and the need to appease the huge Rangers support. It could just be defended on the grounds that Joe Cassidy, fine player though he was for Celtic, was not quite as good as Andy Cunningham, and that if Cunningham were to be included, he would be happier with his mercurial friend Alan Morton rather than the trickier but less familiar Alec Troup.

This held no water whatsoever in the County of Angus, nor indeed in the minds of anyone who had seen the Irish game. A grave injustice was done to Eckie Troup, and he would have to reconcile himself to this for the rest of his footballing career. In the summer of 1921, he would go for walks around his beloved Forfar, graciously admitting that Morton was a great player (Scotland did beat England 3-1 that day and both Cunningham and Morton scored), but if he ever said anything about 'unfair', any wise Forfar sage would have pointed to the hideous jute factories or reminded him of the gravestones erected recently in the local cemetery which mentioned young men who fell at Neuve Chappelle or on the Somme, and said 'Fair, Eckie? Fair? Fa' ever telt ye that life wis gaein to be fair?'

But Eckie was given a chance in the League international on 26 October 1921 at Shawfield, then the home of Clyde. The circumstances of his selection were unusual to say the least. When the team was chosen, Troup would have been disappointed to see the left-wing spot go to Bobby Ferrier of Motherwell. This was not undeserved, for Ferrier was a fine player whose best moments for Motherwell were still to come. The snag, if it could be called that, was that Ferrier was an Englishman, born in Sheffield.

When this was pointed out, some people said that the Scottish League team should be made up of Scotsmen. There was no reason for this, and *The Courier*, although naturally anxious to see a Dundee player in a representative game, had to admit that there were at least two precedents for non-Scotsmen playing for the Scottish League. One was Patsy Gallacher of Ireland in 1913/14 and the other was Dundee's own Herbert Dainty, an Englishman, who had played for the Scottish League *v.* the Southern League in 1911/12.

But the Scottish League, for no apparent reason other than that a League International was now seen as a trial for the 'full' international team, replaced Ferrier with a somewhat embarrassed Troup. Another strange thing happened in this game. A full forty years before substitutes were allowed, the Irish League were allowed to replace the injured Burns of Glenavon by Lyner of Glentoran after the former was badly injured in a collision with Willie McStay of Celtic.

The game, in front of a meagre 12,000 crowd in bad weather, was very one-sided, with the Scottish League winning 3-0, goals coming from Ferguson, Cunningham and Duncan. *The Courier* damned Troup with faint praise. He was 'the most progressive of the line and some of his runs and crosses were quite good, if not up to his usual standard'.

The teams were:

Scottish League: Campbell (Partick Thistle); Birrell (Hearts) and McStay (Celtic); Meiklejohn (Rangers), Cringan (Celtic) and Muirhead (Rangers); Ritchie (Hibs), Cunningham (Rangers), Ferguson (Motherwell), Duncan (Clyde) and Troup (Dundee).

Irish League: Mehaffy (Queen's Island); Savage (Distillery) and Curran (Glenavon); Wallace (Linfield), Scraggs (Glentoran) and Emerson (Glentoran); McGregor (Glentoran), Crooks (Glentoran), Davey (Glentoran), McCracken (Linfield) and Burns (Glenavon).

The first full international of this season (1921/22) was at Wrexham in Wales on 4 February. Troup did not play in this game. That was probably a blessing in disguise, for the game was played in a blizzard, with the ball resembling 'a Christmas pudding' according to some sources. The game itself might well not have been played but for the presence of a trainful of Scottish fans, who might have been sorely disappointed and gave every indication that they might vent their frustration in socially unacceptable

*Scotland v. England at Old Trafford, 17 April 1926. From left to right, back row: Gibson, McMullan, Dougray (referee), Summers, Harper, Cunningham. Front row: Jackson, Gallacher, McStay, Hutton, Thomson, Troup.*

ways. Even the referee himself, the famous Arthur Ward of Kirkham, apparently joined in the clearing of the lines to ensure a start to the game. Scotland lost 1-2.

Whether a fit Troup would have been selected for this game is a moot point, but he was just recovering at this point from a particularly virulent strain of influenza, which may have been a revisitation of the terrible Spanish 'flu which killed so many in the immediate aftermath of the First World War. He had missed a few games for Dundee. But he was back for Dundee on 11 February and had played a few games before the Scottish team for the Ireland game at Celtic Park on 4 March was announced. No excuses of bad conditions were accepted by the Scottish selectors for what was perceived as a disgraceful performance against Wales, a country to whom Scotland had not lost since 1909. Only the back three and centre forward Andy Wilson (now of Middlesbrough rather than Dunfermline) retained their places. This meant a return for Alec Troup.

It was indeed quite a 'hatchet' job done by the Scottish selectors. Apart from the dropping of Alan Morton, which raised the hackles down Ibrox way, three fine players played their one and only game for Scotland that day in the Wrexham snow. They were Michael Gilhooley of Hull City (the only player of that club ever to play for Scotland), Frank Walker of the now defunct Third Lanark and the immensely-talented Will Collier of Raith Rovers. They all had cause to feel ill-treated by the sometimes quixotic Scottish selectors, but the humiliation of losing to Wales was a grievous blow to Scotland's pride, no matter what the circumstances were.

For the Ireland game, Parkhead was the chosen venue (as usual in those days when Ireland were the visitors) for the ill-disguised reason of attracting a large crowd. 50,000 were there that day to see a poor game which Scotland won 2-1. Two goals came from Andy Wilson, to defeat the one by Gillespie of Sheffield United for Ireland.

The reporter of the *Dundee Advertiser* did not enjoy this game. He asked indignantly 'Who was that forlorn figure standing out on the left wing for almost all the game? Why it was Alec Troup, whom Scotland starved of the ball!'. Hinting that inside left Cunningham would have preferred his Rangers colleague Alan Morton, and generally disapproving of Scotland's unimaginative play, the reporter prefers to go into details about the wiles of Celtic's Patsy Gallacher in a losing cause for Ireland rather than dwell on Scotland.

At one point the ball burst when it landed on the top of the perimeter fence. The writer of the *Dundee Advertiser* was quite graphic on this point. '... it expired on the spiked railings – an act of self-immolation performed in disgust'. Leaving aside the point about whether the ball got fed up of the game, other reports do confirm that the game was quite unmemorable and that Scotland were fortunate to win.

Troup did have a 'quiet' game, and only to a point can we agree with the manifestly biased *Dundee Advertiser* that it was because of poor service. In such circumstances, a winger must 'forage', and go and look for the ball. But in view of the lavish praise showered upon Alec's direct opponent, Newcastle's Billy McCracken (and indeed his cousin Robert who played at right half), we must assume that Alec had a game he would rather forget.

The teams were:

Scotland: Campbell (Partick Thistle), Marshall ( Middlesbrough) and McKinlay (Liverpool); Hogg (Ayr United), Cringan (Celtic) and Muirhead (Rangers); Donaldson (Bolton Wanderers), Kinloch (Partick Thistle), Wilson (Middlesbrough), Cunningham (Rangers) and Troup (Dundee).

Ireland: Collins (Celtic), McCracken, W. (Newcastle United) and McCandless (Rangers); McCracken, R. (Crystal Palace), O' Brien (Leicester City) and Emerson (Glentoran); Lacey (Liverpool), Gallacher (Celtic), Irvine (Everton), Gillespie (Sheffield United) and Lyner (Glentoran).

Referee – Mr A. Ward, Kirkham

Alan Morton returned for the England game which Scotland won 1-0 and retained his place for the next few years, however much the Dundee press bleated about it. In fact, Troup never again played for Scotland as a Dundee player. He was transferred to Everton in the early months of 1923, and this was a major setback to Troup's international aspirations. In addition to the fact that Morton continued to play well for both Rangers and Scotland, there was the additional factor that Scotland employed a Home Scots policy in the mid-1920s, meaning that preference was given to those who were plying their trade in Scotland.

This was in some ways a laudable policy. The problem with Anglo-Scots is that they are at the mercy of their English employers, who can some times be none too helpful about releasing them for Scotland commitments. Forty years after Troup's era came a stark demonstration of this. I refer to the distressing events of December 1965 when Scotland needed to beat Italy in Italy to qualify for the 1966 World Cup. English clubs did not release their Anglo-Scots in time, injuries were picked up and Scotland lost.

There were several disturbing aspects of all this. One was the apparent insouciance of the Anglos themselves, who did not appear to want to play for Scotland and generally gave the impression of earning so much money that they didn't care anyway. Another was the fact that the managers of one or two of the clubs were themselves Scotsmen who would on other occasions label themselves as 'proudly patriotic', be interviewed on television with an exaggerated Scottish accent, rolling their 'r's as if they and only they could speak Scots, and say that England were lucky in 1966 to eventually win the World Cup.

This last point was the most hurtful. 1966 was the year Scotland could have won the World Cup. The competition was held in England in conditions conducive to the Scottish game, and Scotland was full of talent in the mid-1960s. 1967 would of course be a great year for Scottish football – Scotland beat England 3-2 at Wembley and Celtic's eleven Scotsmen won the European Cup. Yet, 1966 could have been even better.

All this was forty years after Troup, but it does give some justification for the 'Home Scots only' policy of the mid-1920s. In any case, Home Scots were plentiful and excellent in the 1920s. Those who lament Scotland's inability to qualify for the 2002 World Cup (and other failures) and bleat about the sheer lack of Scottish talent, may well have a point. But it was not always so. In the 1920s, Rangers and Celtic produced great players and were supplemented by teams like Airdrie and Partick Thistle. Famously in 1925, Scotland, captained by Dave Morris of Raith Rovers, beat all three countries.

That same year of 1925 saw economic circumstances deteriorate in Scotland, however, to such an extent that several more players, including captain Morris himself, were compelled to move to England – a serious blow to the fans in Scotland, for given the absence of television, it was then no longer possible to watch such talented Scotsmen. This 'talent drain' also compelled a relaxation of the 'Home Scots only' policy on the part of the Scottish selectors.

But the Scottish success continued. Ireland and Wales were more than competently dispatched in 1925/26, and hopes were high for the game against England on 17 April 1926. There was, however, a problem on the left wing. Alan Morton was suffering long-term injury problems, and had been replaced for the Wales and Ireland matches by Celtic's Adam McLean – a competent substitute, although it is hard to agree with the opinion of quite a few Celtic historians that he was the equal of Morton. But Adam himself picked up an injury in the month of March, and although he was back playing for Celtic in early April, he seemed to have lost a little of his zest and enthusiasm.

It was in these circumstances that the Scottish selectors turned to their forgotten man, Alec Troup, now of Everton. Great was the joy on Merseyside, Dundee and Forfar at the thought that their favourite was to be given another chance. Evertonians, not always loyal 'Englishmen', were delighted that the game would be played at nearby Manchester and quite a few of them would be there – supporting Scotland! Such was their love for the diminutive Alec Troup whom they had taken to their hearts. In addition, there was a dearth of Everton players playing for England, although hopes were being nurtured about a young man called Dean.

1926 was a time of great poverty and labour unrest in Great Britain. There was real trouble in the coalmining industry, and employers with the help of the Baldwin government were bracing themselves for what they feared was to be a Communist insurrection. In fact, it turned out to be a General Strike, which the government won handsomely.

Yet there was some money around as well. Obviously, the rich were very rich and now drove about in motor cars and sailed off to the Riviera in southern France for their holidays, but even for a working-class family, provided the man was in a stable job (and was able to withstand the attractions of alcohol), there were acceptable living standards, if not yet the affluence that was still thirty years in the distance. Yet, for the war widows with children, life continued to be a grossly unequal struggle.

But there were sufficient Scots people with enough money to treat themselves to a weekend in Manchester in 1926. The fact that the game was at Old Trafford rather than the recently-opened Wembley Stadium in London meant that the match was so much nearer, and that an overnight train from Glasgow Central Station was not necessarily out of the pocket of the working man – provided he saved up for it!

Thus it was that 12,000 estimated fans made their way to Manchester. As early as 7.00 a.m., bagpipes were skirling in the centre of Manchester, and respectable middle-class women as well as mill workers were given all sorts of invitations, repeatable and otherwise, by men in kilts. The Germans in the First World War had apparently talked about the 'ladies from hell'; Mancunians now saw them for themselves. One mill girl told the *Glasgow Herald* reporter that she had indeed found out that Scotsmen wore nothing under their kilts, and that she thought the Scottish race were 'absolutely barmy'. Another one thought that one Scotsman looked like Robbie Burns as he sang 'bootiful' songs like 'Mary, my Scots bluebell'. (That particular song was of course Harry Lauder rather than Robbie Burns, but the Lancashire mill girls were flattered by the attention anyway!)

Alec was not part of this early morning revelry, although the Midland Hotel where he had joined the team the night before was all decked in tartan to make them feel at home. Alec enjoyed the opportunity to meet up again with those players he had not seen for some time, particularly the unpretentious Fifer Alec Thomson of Celtic and big Jock Hutton of Aberdeen, with his huge stock of dirty jokes to relieve the tension. Quite a few expressed their regret that the game was not being played at Wembley, for they would have relished a game at the new stadium. Captain Willie McStay held court to journalists, saying that he was quietly confident, but 'quietly' was the key word. The previous week, his own team, Celtic, had lost the Scottish Cup final to St Mirren and he knew all about the dangers of over-confidence.

The teams were:

England: Taylor (Huddersfield Town); Goodall (Huddersfield Town) and Mort (Aston Villa); Edwards (Leeds United), Hill (Burnley) and Green (Sheffield United); York (Aston Villa), Puddlefoot (Blackburn Rovers), Harper (Blackburn Rovers), Walker (Aston Villa) and Ruffell (West Ham United).

Scotland: Harper (Arsenal), Hutton (Aberdeen) and McStay (Celtic); Gibson (Partick Thistle), Summers (St Mirren) and McMullan (Manchester City); Jackson (Huddersfield Town), Thomson (Celtic), Gallacher (Newcastle United), Cunningham (Rangers) and Troup (Everton).

Referee – Mr T. Dougray, Belshill.

To our modern eyes, it seems bizarre that the referee was a Scotsman – the famous Tom Dougray of Belshill, Lanarkshire. Even more incomprehensible was the fact that Mr Dougray did not see anything wrong with having his photograph taken with the Scottish team beforehand! But in the 1920s, this was not considered unusual – Dougray had in fact been the referee in Troup's previous Scotland *v.* England game in 1920. Nor, indeed, did England seem to object to any of his decisions, either in 1920 or in 1926. In the match reports, he was handed the finest compliment of all for a referee – not being mentioned at all!

48,000 packed Old Trafford that day, paying a total of £8,000 for the privilege. The weather was foul, but the rain was easing as the kick-off approached. The heavy ground did have an effect, but it suited Troup who was 'of frequent assistance in carrying out others's [sic] schemes'. The other forwards were outstanding, and the wonder was that Scotland led by only one goal at half time, that scored in the thirty-seventh minute when a pass from Andy Cunningham found Alec Jackson who scored off the post.

In the second half, England mounted a counter-attack with the wind behind them, but they generally 'faltered on the rocks of Hutton, Summers and McStay', and Scotland held out for a famous and deserved victory. For Troup it was probably the highlight of his career (so far) to be on the winning side for Scotland against England. How often he had dreamed of that! The games in Queen Street and the Greens where he had been 'Jimmy Quinn' – how often they had beaten England then! Now it had happened in reality.

That night, there was dancing at the Cross in Forfar when the news came through by the customary telegraph. Erroneous rumours spread that it had been Troup who scored the only goal of the game. The important thing, however, was that Scotland had beaten England again (the fourth time since the war) and this time Forfar had been part of it! It is just a great pity that television was still some thirty years, a Depression and another war away. How they would have enjoyed seeing their Eckie playing for Scotland!

Thus ended the international career of Alec Troup. Alan Morton returned, and Troup, playing in distant Liverpool, faded from the picture. Thus it was that in 1928, Alan Morton played for the Wembley Wizards who beat England 5-1. Troup would certainly have enhanced that game, for 1928 was a great year for him at club level. By the summer of 1929, when Scotland, patronisingly describing themselves as 'missionaries of football' went on a close-season tour of Norway, Germany and Holland, Alan Morton was unavailable for selection. But Alec, aged thirty-four, had now dropped out of the international scene altogether.

*A cartoon from the* Liverpool Echo *during the war years, wanting the star players to be brought back.*

# 10
# THE TWILIGHT OF THE GOD

Alec Troup died in the early hours of 2 January 1952 at his home at Willowbrae, Brechin Road, Forfar, in the presence of his wife, daughter and son-in-law. He had been, as the papers said, 'in indifferent health' for some time. In fact, he died of bronchial carcinoma, or in layman's terms, cancer of the throat. He was fifty-six. Dr Burgess, who had attended Alec during his illness, prescribing painkillers and palliatives to deaden the pain, signed the death certificate.

To say that he was much mourned, missed and lamented by his family and friends and the town itself is to state the obvious. When King George VI died a month later, the grief was hardly more pronounced. Alec Troup remained the unpretentious, loveable man that he always had been. In his later years, he would be seen taking his walk on a Sunday, nodding and smiling to everyone and small boys would be told 'that man played for Scotland'. It was hard to find anyone with a bad word to say about him.

On a personal note, the author has the vaguest recollection of an autumn Sunday afternoon in 1951 in what is commonly known as the Jail Road, but is officially termed Market Street. At the age of three, one is perhaps less impressed by people who had played for Scotland than one should be, but the kindly Alec, by now an ill man, tipped his broad-brimmed hat, said a few words to mother and father (who were clearly in awe and reverence of the man) then bent down to ask after the health of the three year old. 'That man played for Scotland!' was a phrase that one recalls being mentioned again and again.

Alec's niece, Betty Piggott, would recall how popular he was with children, for he was always cheery, had a fund of stories, was a 'laugh a minute' and was an excellent Santa Claus at Christmas parties. He was a teetotaller, a non-smoker, and would never seek the limelight. Quite a few ex-footballers have been known to boast and exaggerate their exploits. Not so Alec. He would be willing to talk with everyone, and would talk about his career if asked, but he never pushed himself forward. He didn't need to, for he had done more or less everything he wanted to in the football world. He drove an Austin car, then later a Hillman, and on a summer day loved to visit the beautiful Angus glens like Glen Clova and Glen Prosen.

Another niece, May Stewart (née Troup), the daughter of his brother David, tells of how shy a man he was, and his shyness was one of the reasons why he was very happy to stay in the background in his shop rather than serve people! In the house, he walked around quietly on his tiptoes, lest he disturb anyone! Yet his quiet demeanour was never to be mistaken for weakness, for he was a strong character, devoted to his wife who was quite happy to call him by his football nickname 'Troupie'.

*'The Elder Statesman'. A photograph taken in the late 1940s.*

# EVERTON FOOTBALL CLUB CO. LTD

*Telephone*
AINTREE 2263

GENERAL MANAGER
C. S. BRITTON

GROUND & REGISTERED OFFICE:
GOODISON PARK
**LIVERPOOL·4**

*Telegrams*
FOOTBALL LIVERPOOL

SECRETARY
W DICKINSON

OUR REF
WD/JM

YOUR REF

DATE
3rd January 1952.

Mrs. Troup,
Willow Brae,
Brechin Road,
Forfar.

Dear Mrs. Troup,

My Directors were very grieved to learn of
the great loss you have sustained in the death of
Alex and they have asked me to convey to you their
sincere sympathy.

Alex was held in great esteem by all who
know him at Goodison Park, and his loss will be keenly
felt by all.

Yours sincerely,

*W. Dickinson*

On the family front, he had seen his daughter Nan grow up into an attractive young lady and was very proud to lead her down the aisle at the Old Kirk on 9 June 1950 to be married to a man called George Taylor. In the fullness of time, his only grandson, Brian, would be born on 31 March 1951, but sadly, illness would prevent Alec from seeing too much of him.

When he finished his playing career in 1933, Alec had opted to stay in his beloved Forfar. He was like the many Forfarians who would return from all sorts of adventures – from slave trading in the eighteenth century, from the Crimea, Afghanistan or South Africa in the nineteenth and Flanders or North Africa in the twentieth and say of his beloved soil 'This is a braw place!'. Or as Sir Walter Scott would have put it:

*Alec in his retirement from football and the proud owner of an Austin Seven.*

*After retirement! Alec plays for a Dundee Veterans team in a charity match at Muirton Park, Perth. From left to right, back row: Thomson (linesman), McLean, Lindsay, Brownlie, Nicoll, Bain. Front row: Henderson, Fleming, Hart, Bell, Irving, Troup. Two other Forfarians are here, Davie McLean (ex-Celtic) and George Henderson (ex-Rangers).*

Breathes there the man with soul so dead
Who never to himself hath said
This is my own, my native land!

The Forfar in which Alec died in 1952 was of course a vastly different place to that in which he was born in 1895. There still remained the jute factories with their long, monotonous hours of work and the dreadful houses with outside toilets, but a start had been made to create in Forfar, as elsewhere in the United Kingdom, a Welfare State in which everybody had a fair deal. The Labour government of 1945 to 1951 had now eliminated the worst excesses of capitalism. Healthcare in particular, under the vigorous stewardship of the dynamic Nye Bevan, was seen as a priority, with every baby getting free milk.

That this change in society would be permanent was made obvious after the Conservatives returned to power in 1951. The Prime Minister, Sir Winston Churchill himself, anything but a socialist, nevertheless said things like 'I can think of no finer investment than putting milk into babies!' and tacitly accepted the reforms that Labour had brought. Less pleasant than milk but no less beneficial to the youngsters were the vaccinations against such diseases as diphtheria, polio and tuberculosis.

Overseas, the threat of German expansionism, which had raised its head twice during that half century, had now gone. No more would Forfar women lament the loss of those who had died on some foreign field. There still remained places like Korea, but that was far away. Russia was seen as some sort of a threat but to a Forfarian, the Cold War was something waged every January and involved having sufficient coal for the fire!

The town was returning to prosperity following the bad days of the 1930s, with their short time working and brutal, repressive employers. Jute factories were now back to a forty-five hour week – every day beginning at 6.00 a.m. for a three-hour shift, then breakfast from 9 until 10, work again from 10 a.m. to 1 p.m., then the 'diethoor' – the diet hour or lunch break, then 2 p.m. to 5 p.m. – and rationing, that necessary curse of the war years and immediate aftermath was on the way out. Goods were becoming plentiful again, and more importantly, the workers had the money with which to buy them.

On the football field, Alec continued to be interested in the fortunes of his three fomer teams. Like many an old player, watching perhaps did not always come easily to him, but he was frequently seen at Station Park, where he would have seen Forfar in 1949 winning the 'C' Division of the Scottish League and earning promotion to the 'B' Division. He would have thrilled by the play of Tommy Adams and Jimmy Caskie (both greats of the game who had been prevailed upon to play the last years of their careers with Forfar) but no doubt he would look at his old pal and fellow Scottish internationalist Davie McLean and shake his had sadly in agreement as Davie said 'Aye, but they're no as guid as we were, Alec'. Sadly, his old boss and mentor, James Black, died, a few months before Alec did.

One particular game in September 1951 would have stirred up memories. Alec's health was failing fast, but he still managed to attend the League Cup quarter final between Forfar Athletic and Celtic. Celtic had won the first leg at Parkhead comfortably, and the second leg at Station Park was little other than a glorified friendly, but Forfar did well to earn a draw. Alec would have recalled that previous time that the mighty Celts came to town – the game that made him when he taught Sunny Jim a thing or two about football and earned the approval of the great McMenemy! On that occasion in 1951, Celtic's manager, the great and gentle Jimmy McGrory (who of course had played against Troup in the early 1930s) on hearing of Alec's failing health, sought him out in the old stand before the game and had a long chat about old times.

Alec would also occasionally visit Dens Park. Dundee had a fine team in the late 1940s and early 1950s, and Alec would have enjoyed the sight of some fine players like the half-back line of Gallacher, Cowie and Boyd, but he would have gasped in anguish as his old team had the chance to win the League title on the last day of the 1949 season at Falkirk, but for some unaccountable reason blew it. Nevertheless, a year later they bought Billy Steel from Derby County and were rewarded in October 1951 when they won the Scottish League Cup for the first time. Sadly by that time, Alec would probably have been too ill to have travelled to Hampden, but he undoubtedly listened to it on the wireless.

Everton were less successful in the late 1940s. The 1930s had seen an FA Cup triumph in 1933 and a League championship the year previously, both of which owed a great deal to Alec's old friend Dixie Dean. In 1938, Everton played in Scotland in the Empire Exhibition Trophy, a one-off competition for the best in Scotland and England. Sadly for the Toffees, they lost in the final to Celtic, but in the last peacetime season of 1939, they lifted the League Championship to finish the 1930s on a high note. Their many supporters were quick to remind anyone that they met during the Second World War that Everton were the 'real' Champions of England, irrespective of who won the numerous 'Mickey Mouse' wartime competitions!

Alec had earned enough money from his footballing career to be reasonably well off, although he was hardly in the superstar category of those who came along after him. Being a shrewd character, Alec had long ago invested some of his money in his draper's business in Castle Street, although he employed his sister-in-law to run it for him. He also still practised his trade as a plasterer from his yard in Queen Street. He sold his draper's shop some time before the start of Second World War, thinking correctly that the onset of war with its inevitable consequences of rationing of things like clothes would devastate his business. In any case, it was not a trade that he was all that interested in. But he did enjoy his plastering, (no doubt immune through time to all the jokes about plastering around) and he kept that business going, being proud to describe himself on his daughter's marriage certificate as a 'master plasterer'.

During the Second World War, he was also quite happy to be described as a munitions worker. A bus-load of workers travelled daily to Brechin to work for the Coventry Gauge and Tool Company, and Alec was one of them. This company made all sorts of things for the war effort and Alec worked at a milling machine, but it was too big for him and he had to stand on a box! At lunchtimes he would be begged to tell tales of his footballing career, delighting the young apprentices, and he was even prevailed upon from time to time to play football for the milling section against other

*Football runs in the blood! Forfar West End in 1975 contains Alec's grandson, Brian Taylor (second from right in the front row).*

parts of the factory. He was in his late forties by this time, but Allan Stewart recalls how well he played. 'He just put a foot on the ball and did his trickery and once in the clear would sent over inch-perfect crosses to the far post, a joy to see.'

In his last years, he would often be seen on his walks with his dog, Ben. Always well-dressed and thoroughly deserving of the word dapper to describe him, he would go on walks up the Balmashanner hill (commonly known as Bummie to the locals) or round the loch. He was always polite, courteous and humble. He knew he had been a foot-baller and a good one, but that did not make him one iota better than anyone else. He was not really a religious man, but did put in the occasional appearance at the Old Kirk of a Sunday. Like many an ex-serviceman, he was particularly careful to attend church on Remembrance Sunday.

Like most football players, he carried the scars of his profession with him. He had a stud mark on his brow, his shoulder still tended to dislocate if he had lifted anything or had done anything particularly strenuous and occasionally his knees would give him problems. He was prone to bouts of sciatica in winter, but never lapsed into self pity or blamed it all on anyone else.

The problem with his shoulder, which had troubled him repeatedly throughout his career, stayed with him to his death. It seemed to be was a weak joint which dislocated very easily. As a protection against it happening, he would often take to the field with his shoulder strapped up. If it did happen during a game, it was usually easy enough to sort. He could massage it back in, or he could even lie down on a table or a floor and manipulate his chest and arm until the reassuring click was heard. Curiously, this problem seems to be genetic, for although his daughter and grandson did not have this problem, his great-grandson Greg does.

In footballing terms, Alec was a real 'winger' – a term which has sadly passed out of use. The author is unashamedly nostalgic for the days of the brown ball, the referee wearing black, the goalkeepers with yellow polo neck jersey and nothing ridiculous like the number thirty-five written on the back! In Alec's day, every team had five forwards – an outside right, inside right, centre forward, inside left and outside left. The two outside men were often small, tricky and frequently the victims of rough treatment from burly full backs, but the crowd loved to watch the way that, using every inch of the park, they would take on and skin their opponents to send over inch-perfect crosses for the centre forward to score. Alec, of course, started off as an inside left, and even a left half before that, but it was as a left winger that he made his mark.

The skills lay in dribbling, beating opponents, reaching the dead ball line and crossing. It was the sort of thing that crowds loved. Great wingers of the past included men like Alan Morton of Rangers, Stanley Matthews of Blackpool, Tom Finney of Preston North End, Jimmy Johnstone of Celtic and Garrincha of Brazil. The author would not hesitate for a moment to put forward the name of Alec Troup in that pantheon.

It might well be asked why he is not better known. There are several answers to this question, the obvious one being that he came at the same time as Alan Morton who was at least his equal and possessed the advantage of playing for Rangers, a factor which certainly weighed heavily on Scottish selectors. In addition, Alec would never put himself forward. He was shy, retiring and content with his lot, lacking perhaps a little of the 'devil' which is necessary. He was a small-town boy, more than happy to return to his roots after his career was over.

There were perhaps two factors that persuaded him not to go into football management. One was that he was all too aware that, even in the 1930s, life as a manager was tough and precarious. He did not fancy the sack just because somebody missed a penalty! Far better to retire to private life with his own fairly secure business in the town where he was born and which he loved.

In addition, Alec was simply not nasty enough to be a manager. Managers do on occasion have to do things that they would prefer not to. They have to drop a favourite of theirs if the press and fans are on their back, they have to tell a young player that his services are being dispensed with simply because he is not good enough and they have to, on occasion, go along with a few pieces of sharp practice in order to obtain that all-important commodity called success. Alec was simply not cut out for this job, and he had enough self-awareness to realise it.

It was some time in 1951 that he saw Dr Burgess in St James's Terrace (or the Back Sides as it was commonly known) about some problem in his throat. It seemed to be blocked and he occasionally had difficulty swallowing. Tests would show that it was cancer, too far progressed for any surgery. He had a matter of months to live.

He did not want a fuss made of him, and would have preferred no one to know. But Forfar people have a way of finding out about such things, particularly in the case of such a famous and well-respected little man. He was well nursed by the woman who had loved him, and there was a certain quiet dignity about the way that he went. He saw in the New Year of 1952, but only just.

The day of his funeral, Friday 4 January 1952, was a cold, snowy one. Snow had disrupted quite a few of the New Year holiday fixtures, and the thaw would not arrive until the night of Alec's funeral. The bad weather probably put off some of his old companions and rivals from travelling some distance, otherwise Patsy Gallacher (himself now a sick man) from Glasgow and many others would have attended.

As it was, *The Courier* reports that his old friend Davie McLean was there, as were Jock Thomson and Davie Raitt, both ex-Dundee and Everton players. Willie Cook, George Henderson and Sam Irving were also there, as were a shoal of people representing all the local junior teams. The service at the house and the cemetery was conducted by Reverend D.M. Bell, minister of Forfar Old Kirk. Dundee FC and Everton FC both sent a wreath.

There may have been someone else as well. The railway workers from Forfar were returning home that evening on the 3.30 p.m. train from Aberdeen. The train was a few minutes late after ploughing its way through the snow. The train stopped at Forfar Station and as the workers disembarked, a few passengers went to get on the train which was heading towards Perth and the south. One of these passengers, a tall man in his late forties, perhaps, with a slightly swarthy complexion, held open a door to allow a woman with a pram to get on board. He had obviously been at Troup's funeral, for he was wearing a black tie. He nodded to the workers and remarked on the dreadful weather in an English accent, with a northern, Lancashire sort of dialect. One of the workers who had spent the war years in the RAF identified it as Liverpudlian. Sadly, the train was pulling out of Forfar Station before the penny dropped as to who the man was. It was none other than the great Dixie Dean, departing anonymously after paying his respects to the man who had made him what he was.

On the following day, Saturday 5 January, a one-minute silence was held at Dundee *v.* Hearts, Forfar *v.* Stenhousemuir and quite a few other grounds as well. Those who stood bareheaded in the rain that day realised that a great talent had departed, and that there would never be another Eckie Troup.